The Pot and the Knife

JOHN DRURY

The Pot and the Knife

SCM PRESS LTD

© John Drury 1979

334 01275 9

First published 1979
by SCM Press Ltd,
58 Bloomsbury Street, London

Typeset by Input Typesetting Ltd
and printed in Great Britain by
Richard Clay Ltd,
Bungay, Suffolk

To Geoffrey Lampe

Contents

What the pot does is to reflect the cupped hand. . . And nothing has been discovered about nature herself when man imposes these warm, rounded, feminine, artistic shapes on her. The only thing you reflect is the shape of your own hand.

But there is another action of the human hand which is different and opposite. That is the splitting of wood or stone; for by that action the hand (armed with a tool) probes and explores beneath the surface, and thereby becomes an instrument of discovery. There is a great intellectual step forward when man splits a piece of wood, or a piece of stone, and lays bare the print that nature had put there before he split it.

J. Bronowski, *The Ascent of Man*

If it were not for the Poetic or Prophetic character the Philosophic or Experimental would soon be at the ratio of all things, and stand still, unable to do other than repeat the same dull round over again.

William Blake, *There is no Natural Religion*

Foreword

In the winter of 1978 I was Fleck Resident in Religion at Bryn Mawr in Pennsylvania, an academic-cum-pastoral post founded by Admiral and Mrs Fleck in memory of their daughter Roian. There the ideas in this book had their first integrated airing; if they have changed since then it has not been out of all recognition, and without that opportunity they would not have got far at all. I am very grateful for it and all the kindness that went with it.

Before that some of them had been explored in articles in *The Modern Churchman*, *Theology* and *Crucible*. But apart from the section about beauty from *Theology* October 1973 they have been broken up and recast or reset. I owe much to meetings where connections between faith, practice and criticism have been discussed in different ways and in which I have been lucky to be involved: editorial meetings for *Theology* with my colleagues David Jenkins and James Mark and, in correspondence, with contributors to the magazine; the Bishop of Southwark's 'Caps and Mitres'; the Clerical Boat Club at which Norfolk clergymen meet and talk with the greatest freedom; a discussion group, mainly of dons, in the University of East Anglia, and seminars there; the Doctrine Commission of the Church of England; the Loddon Rural Deanery Chapter; the clergy and congregation of Norwich Cathedral; various groups in East Anglia under the aegis of the Cambridge University Extra-Mural Board. The list is neither complete nor in any order of significance.

I am grateful to Laurence Pollinger Ltd and the Estate

of the late Mrs Frieda Lawrence Ravagli for permission to quote from *Phoenix* and *The Complete Poems of D. H. Lawrence*.

Besides all this, I would like to record some more personal debts. To the clergyman at a King's Lynn lecture course who told me that God was both more immanent and more transcendent than is generally supposed (he has since become a social worker). To the Revd John Bowden and the Revd Dr Arthur Peacocke, who persuaded me that a Mozartian could attend to Wagner. To the Very Revd Alan Webster, who showed me that an old ecclesiastical set-up could still make itself useful to people. To Canon Peter Bradshaw for a memorable sermon about God. To Jean Cooper for typing and retyping. To Dennis Nineham for rubbing my nose in the elements of rigorous theological criticism. To my wife above all for a wonderful combination of analytical skill and comforting reassurance, and to our children for making me think about the future of Christianity.

Norwich
Easter 1979

Introduction

Since this book does not fall neatly into any of the usual sub-divisions of Christian theology which give the reader some idea of what he is on to, a descriptive introduction is necessary to make amends.

It is not apologetic, though it continually tries to link specifically Christian with other interests. It is not historical criticism, though it depends on its methods. It is not spirituality because, though the discovery of the inner life of Christianity is its aim, it is too argumentative and discursive to be directly useful for prayer. It is something of a mixture of the three, attempting so to manage the engagement of critical with spiritual concerns as to yield some sense comprehensible beyond the bounds and language-games of conscious Christianity.

Since I wrote *Angels and Dirt*, which was spirituality, the pressures of criticism have born more strongly on me through my New Testament work and the present theological climate. I have also been more fully and widely involved in church life than before. So I wanted to return to the area explored in that earlier book with an increased sense of these pressures and write a more ascetic general book which goes a bit further into the traditional centre of Christianity. The result is really about something subsidiary to the usual sub-divisions and to the life of the church: the tangled and indissoluble relations of criticism and creativity, of the analytical and poetic faculties. Hence the title and the two quotations which come before the Foreword. I do not hope to have got these relations right.

The areas in which they happen are too spacious, intricate and explosive for that. But I have tried to get them on to speaking terms with one another at a few points because I believe this to be desperately important for the future of Christianity. If it is to be creative enough to justify its role as a religion of universal salvation, and not decline into a sectarian enclave, it has to go through the fires of criticism and not skirt round them. This is not an arbitrary ordeal. The critical questions are basic common-sense questions and there is an alliance between the professors at their desks and people in their pews or pubs which unfortunately often goes over the head, or between the feet, of official and institutional religion. Yet it must be possible to be a Christian without thinking and living in an utterly, and so irrelevantly, odd way. To put it in traditional theological terms, there must be a grace which perfects nature rather than abolishing it. It is not cheap. The price is the status which preserves the church as a thing apart. But if this is a declining asset, it is a bargain.

Inevitably the discussion takes on the question of myth at an early stage. It is an awkward word. It has a pejorative sense in the street and a neutrally descriptive one in the study. I use the latter, while trying to give room to the sense of distrust (but not the dismissiveness) in the former. It covers a very wide field or spectrum of material. Although this is a nuisance which future refinements may abate, I have not found it possible at present to do otherwise. Myth is indispensable to Christianity. Our main problem at the moment is not that we have it, but that we keep it wrapped up in a napkin and it does not work well enough. To get it going again, it has to be taken through the analytical fires and not kept away from them. Again, there is a price. Myth loses the unquestioned privilege of subjective domination which it enjoyed so long as it was not distinguished from fact and history. But there is a benefit, too: the freedom which comes with interested detachment and can be called love. Myth is made for man and not man for myth.

Similar things happen in the subsequent discussion of

other topics. Symbols are indispensable, too, but also need critical evaluation and servicing if they are to serve and gear in to the changing conditions of life as they should. Some time-honoured ones need treatment, more or less thorough-going, some are fine as they are and some may be redundant. The art is in choosing and the timing of the choosing. The myths, symbols and doctrines by which the central figure of Christ is known and presented can only be kept away from this at a cost in intelligibility. And to be intelligible we have to choose: always a choice 'for the time being' in a radical sense of the phrase, but always inescapable too if survival in a more than formal sense is the name of the game. So the last two chapters present the individual, the basic Christian and human unit, thinking and living his Christianity at certain key-points of experience, finding a gospel that more than survives – clarifies, subdues and saves – in the critical interaction between faith and life in its ordinary colours.

1

The Self-denying Centre

❧

The religious experience of humanity is at any time more widespread than the area covered by any single religious organization and more diverse than it can cope with while remaining decently organized. That has, so far as we know, always been the case, but now we know it even more thoroughly than in the heyday of religious pluralism in the Greek and Roman world. This problem of an *embarras de richesses*, so great that it threatens chaos, is met by emphasizing a central idea from among the rest round which everything can cluster. The difficulty is to find a centre which is, even temporarily, both hospitable enough to embrace the richness and definite enough to have some organized shape.

The Pharisees of Jesus' day, their predecessors and followers (the rabbis), are a case in point. From the welter of diverse experience which made up Judaism, and which was already enshrined by being written down in an extraordinarily diverse collection of scriptures, they chose the one majestic principle of Law or Torah. Everything else found its place around that. As such choices go, it was a good one. The theme of the covenant, a legal nexus of moral demand and obedience, had been hammered out by the prophets, worked on in books such as Exodus, Leviticus, Numbers and Deuteronomy, and it permeated the historical books – most blatantly, Chronicles. But it was not quite good enough. It had to be stretched by energetic special pleading. All Scripture was Law. Or was it? The Song of Songs was a pastoral love lyric. But it was scripture and scripture was Law, *ergo* it was really about the covenant relation of God and Israel which, after all, the prophets had explored in sexual terms. A trickier problem was posed by Genesis, because it is all about those primeval patriarchs who had wandered here and there and been *en rapport* with God before the Law was given on Mount Sinai. Their.wanderings were a response to moral demand, but of a simple kind. Amplification was needed to vindicate the principle that Law was 'it'. The patriarchs *must* have obeyed it in some detail, so books such as Jubilees were written to show them doing this. That this approach does not just belong to the historical museum or lumber room is shown by an incident from a contemporary Jewish seminar. An ortho-dox student, expecting the answer 'yes', had asked the question whether the patriarchs wore hats. Scepticism raised its head. The student pleaded in aid Genesis 32.1: 'Jacob went on his way and the angels of God met him.' The bafflement of his colleagues was met by his trium-phant conclusion, 'Would our father Jacob have gone on his way *and* met angels without his hat on?' The point, of course, is not so silly or superficial as the story. Ordering power is got by extending the argument in a way which is not just special pleading but also the introduction of a fiction which is satisfying because, in terms of the central concern, it is apt and homogeneous. Then it is bent round into a circle. A ring is forged out of the nugget of gold which is the central principle of Law. The change in metaphor, from nugget to ring, is inevitable, creative and ominous. It has to be done to create intelligible order, but a price is paid in the doing of it. There is a loss of undifferentiated innocence in the interests of a conscious clarity. And however much this is done to include as much experience as possible, it cannot help excluding much of it, too. By becoming circular it makes a difference between those who are happy and consciously satisfied to live within the ring and those who are not. This perennial difficulty with circular arguments can only be escaped with the breaking of the ring by a stronger spiritual force.

The Christians offered another centre which, at least

momentarily, did this. Jesus the Messiah fulfilled the Law, achieved its end – in both senses of 'end' – by realizing the immediate presence of God which it circled about. The Law was thus broken, dethroned and relativized. The nugget (or 'the pearl of great price') superseded the ring. But could it last like that? The Christians were liberated from one set of problems and themes for special pleading but were soon in much the same difficulty, and dealt with it not so differently. They soon found themselves at the ambiguous but inevitable business of forging the ring. Jesus Christ had to be everything. Ends had to meet. Christ was universal fulfilment. All the scriptures pointed to him. Or did they? Only if a secret meaning, expressed in apt fictions, was discovered in most of them. The results could be startlingly ironical – to us, though not to the people who used this approach. Jesus was no cleric. He was hostile to the higher clergy and they returned the attitude – with equal force at least. Yet for the writer of the Epistle to the Hebrews he was the great and ultimate High Priest of the Old Testament's cultic laws.

There was imaginatively creative aptness here in the exposition of Jesus's atoning work, but also a certain historical absurdity. There is another and more recent example. Christians valiantly and energetically concerned with the liberation of humanity, and not afraid of taking their concern into the determinative arena of politics, have appealed to Jesus as the author and pioneer of such secular salvation. They joined their religious and political concerns. Edward Norman, in his 1978 Reith Lectures, called this into question with unwelcome force. Was Jesus such a political activist? The Zealots were, but we have no record of his joining them. Rather, we have abundant testimony in the gospels, John's above all,[1] of his concern for the standing of the individual in the face of God. But even here we cannot rest. Norman prised Jesus away from the grasp of modern ideologists in order to make him the exemplar of the kind of religion he himself prefers, a profound and fervid pietism in which human worthlessness is dazzled by transcendent grace. How does this sort with the gospels? Not so very well either. For there we read of a Jesus who was content to heal people's diseases and send them back to ordinary life, to treat forgiveness as an everyday duty rather than a shattering religious experience, to proclaim the kingdom of God in the social and natural everyday.

A religion needs a centre to give shape to the volatile variety of the experiences to which it appeals. By more or less creative special pleading it stretches and forges itself to cover things which it approves but which often did not originally have much to do with it. As soon as this special pleading is spotted by people who are not interested in its object, and also have religious concerns which are ignored or crowded out by its circularity, there is a squabble. The unifying device becomes a source of division and a whirlpool of aggression. And so things go on and on, with religion quarrelsomely turned in on itself, having less and less to impress or help humanity at large, until the ring is broken – but only to be refashioned. People who are actively concerned with a sublime ideal are inveterately quarrelsome. Politicians and writers, healers and musicians, have their own versions of the same dilemma and the high-minded bitchiness it entails. Like Christians, they too are frustrated by it and ashamed of it, if they have the leisure and detachment to notice it, and cannot stop it. They, too, have to forge rings in order to be intelligible, and have to pay the price of excluding where they meant to include. So, what? Usually cynicism: the stately, sometimes even heroic, expression of despair. There is, however, the hope and possibility of something else. At this point a gospel could engage and break the circle if only such a gospel were available. It needs to be something more than religion as so far achieved and organized. It will even have to be something opposed to the confidence mixed with possessive restlessness of such religion, if it is to save religious people from the tight circles their religions get them into. If it posits a centre, as religions apparently have to do, it will have to be not just majestically clear and hospitable but also a *self-denying centre*. It will have to be a centre at which breaking and giving away is at least as permanently at work as joining and holding. There is an image of it in the central Christian rite of Holy Communion: the focal 'body' of Christ broken and given. For all its security of being officially there, it will be alien and hostile both to religious confidence and religious despair.

If anything has happened to the reader by now, it will be boredom with the words 'religion' and 'religious'. If so, let him hold on to it for a while because it could be the 'specifically creative boredom' to which G. F. Woods referred at a similar point in the argument of his *A Defence of Theological Ethics*.[2] 'At least,' he said, 'I may have made you thoroughly tired of the word "standard". This would be progress, because I believe that one of the most effective factors in the progress of philosophical theology is the promotion of sheer boredom with any traditional or contemporary jargon.' Beneath the level of words used as counters in arguments, there can be little doubt that institutional religion has also, by becoming obsessive, become a bore – to many who practise it as much as to many more who do not. The situation is not unprecedented. The good pagan Celsus reacted similarly, in the second century, when presented with yet another – Christianity. What was so exceptional about it a time when the eastern Mediterranean was swarming with people 'who wander about begging both inside and outside temples (!) and frequent both cities and camps on the pretence of prophesying. And any one of them is ready and accustomed to say "I am the God", or, "a son of God", or, "a divine spirit" and, "I have come, for the world is already on the point of destruction and you, O men, will perish for your injustice. But I wish to save you, and you will see me again returning with heavenly power. Blessed is he who has worshipped me now" '?[3] Then as now[4] there was no shortage of rings for sale, of self-authenticated revelations of the divine calling for attention to themselves as the one thing needful – in the streets and squares of provincial towns as well as in the established shrines. Arresting, in an inconclusive way, to those of no religion and embarrassing to the devotees of other ones, to the disciplined and reflective mind they were and are a bore – yet another?

And what *is* so exceptional about Christianity? Faced with this question the first Christian apologists made two mistakes which are still made today, both of them circular arguments with a vengeance. One was to ask, what was so problematical about Christianity in such a setting? Here is the engineer hoist with his own petard, blown up by his own bomb. In his efforts to sell his uniquely effective product he makes it equal with the rest of the market. Immediately he lurches the other way. The other options are frauds, appropriately presented in fraudulent myths. Here is the real and supreme article, presented in what might be mistaken for myths but are really divinely authenticated revelatory facts. This self-advertising claim to uniqueness is one of the banalities of religions. It is felt to be essential, for how could one commit oneself to a religion while seeing that it is one among others, that it is relative? Yet *cosi fan tutte*, that's what they all do and, in terms of the opera of that name, they virtually ask for a debunking and demythologizing Don Alfonso to puncture their inflated (they would say, inspired) claims and bring them down to reality. It is precisely here, nearer to Don Alfonso than to the ecstatically idolizing lovers whom he opposes, that a gospel impinges and the saving play begins. It is a Christian gospel, for me *the* Christian gospel which this book is about and which has already been glimpsed in Jesus as the breaker of the ring and in the ritual rehearsing of breaking and giving in Holy Communion. Further exploration and explanation of it is offered in the pages which follow. For the moment it is worth noticing the hopeful appropriateness of it to a religion which originates with a severe critic of organized religion, and which is at present being subjected to severe doses of criticism of its doctrinal and institutional achievements.

This theme of the positively helpful contribution of criticism to a creative, religiously self-denying gospel was grasped and explored, intuitively but elusively, in a letter written by Dietrich Bonhoeffer to his friend Bethge from his cell in the Nazi prison at Tegel on 30 April 1944:[5] four urgent pages which are of more consequence to Christianity nowadays than volumes of systematic theology. 'You would be surprised,' he wrote, 'and perhaps even worried by my theological thoughts and the conclusions that they lead to.' The warning was necessary, because Bonhoeffer posed the apparently innocuous question 'what Christianity really is, or indeed who Christ really is, for us today?', and then answered it from within the devastating conviction that 'people as they are now simply cannot be religious any more'.

The exploration which follows is notoriously episodic and teasing, but themes which are integral to it have already shown their faces in this chapter, not least that our salvation nowadays necessitates something other than the usual religious ploys, remedies, and tangles. His first step is to establish this as a matter of fact rather than regret. He is no more impressed than Celsus by religious goings-on, but more impressively unimpressed because he is a believer inside, and not just a critic outside. 'If one day (and it is clear enough that for Bonhoeffer himself that day has already dawned) it becomes clear that the "religious *a priori*" (the conviction that people are religious) does not exist at all, but was a historically conditioned and transient form of human self-expression. . . – what does that mean for "Christianity"? It means that the foundation is taken away from the whole of what has up to now been our "Christianity", and that there remain only a few "last survivors of the age of chivalry", or a few intellectually dishonest people, on whom we can descend as "religious". Are they to be the chosen few?'

In a few lines Bonhoeffer has grasped the full effect of modern critical methods, as used by historians and sociologists, on Christianity. They do not go down on their knees and drop their tools in the face of anything. They work on into the Bible, the creeds and the whole sacred apparatus, giving secular, or quite ordinary, explanations of them which are intelligible and acceptable. They break things up as they go. It is like a sea eating away at a holy island where people came to worship, not to criticize. Those who remain on it, 'the Christians, a

declining band',[6] are living in the past, romantic if they
were not so shabby.

Then 'how do we speak in a "secular" way about
"God"?' Creativity is harder than criticism and satire. It
must be done by church people 'not regarding ourselves
. . . as specially favoured, but rather as belonging to the
whole world'. At this point the strict negatives begin, but
only begin, to turn to the positive: a Christ 'no longer an
object of religion, but something quite different, really the
Lord of the whole world. But what does that mean?' It
takes a long postscript for him to say and the negatives
keep coming back. 'Religious people speak of God when
human knowledge has come to an end, or when human
resources fail – in fact it is always the *deus ex machina* that
they bring on to the scene.' They 'reserve some space for
God'. But this is hopeless. We must look instead for
'religionless Christianity' – and there Bonhoeffer leaves us
with 'all the very best!'

What are we to make of Bonhoeffer's daunting and
indispensable legacy? At the very least he has blown a
hole in the problem which allows some sort of escape and
promises that it will not be away from Christ but towards
him. Christ as the privileged centre of a religion, the
apogee of the unique, if circular, rightness which all people
and all religions long to possess and claim or pretend they
have, that is left aside. Christ as 'really the Lord of the
world', that is promised. How do we move from the one
to the other, from the negative to the positive? Perhaps
Bonhoeffer gave us enough hints after all. The eating of
secularism into religion, though resisted by the 'last
survivors of the age of chivalry', is assisted from another
direction by the energy of a gospel about the self-denying
descent of the privileged divine into 'a historically
conditioned and transient form of human self-expression'.
This is to present a doctrine of incarnation which is
thorough-going at the point where traditional orthodoxy
demurs and qualifies, restores to the self-denying divine
being the privileged and 'special' attributes which he
abandoned 'for us men and for our salvation'. Compared
with the nice equipoise of death and glory, descent and

ascent, in orthodox belief it is lop-sided. But it is lop-sided in the direction which leads to some escape and progress from religion's ancient bind of offering universal salvation on privileged terms, of making universal God into a tribal totem. And we cannot cope with everything at once. The trick is to find the tool for the moment, and then the rest may be added to us. It could be this force in early Christianity, exemplified by Jesus and Paul, which secularized religion, by breaking the boundaries of the privileged enclave, and discovering God in the whole world. Christians did it by positing a new centre, universally inclusive and without privilege, in Jesus Christ. It could not stay like that for ever or for long. People cannot for ever keep breaking through. They need to establish themselves and make boundaries to live in. This need was there all the time, an awkward bed-fellow for the universal scope which, tragically, it did not mean to diminish but only to establish. It gathered force as the church took the necessary but ominous steps of getting a theology of itself and defining its teaching. The force which we resort to, then, is not all that there is to be said about Christianity. But if we are not to stand paralysed in our crucial situation (hoping like the white South African régimes that by some miracle or trick we may yet keep everything), then we must choose. And this, for the time being, seems to be the Christian thing to choose: in the faith that, if so, then the rest will some day be added to us, and the godly fear that if we do not, it will not.

It is the best bet – remembering that in religion the word 'bet' is not far from the vital commitment of faith which dares to choose – to act against our inclination to hoard, sit tight and never choose. But faith is not intellectual suicide. Though it makes an imaginative jump ahead of the intellect, it gets from the intellect all the help it can in deciding which way to jump. The choice for the gospel of the self-denying centre, of the God self-divested of privilege in order to be thoroughly in the world, is backed by criticism – as the best choices always are. For criticism pushes the same way. We posit the anxious and all-important question 'can we have a religion which does not claim special privilege for something?' Criticism, using language familiar to faith, replies that it must be this or nothing. It will not down tools at the crucial point because the ground whereon it stands, christology or whatever, is holy. It has to be faithful to itself if it is to be honest and faithful to God. But – and here is its enlightening and Christian point – this refusal to preserve the divine by calling a halt to human knowledge, to locate God where it comes to an end, can be and historically has been rewarded by finding God in unprivileged everything. This was Bonhoeffer's point, and the point of William Blake's onslaught on institutional religion in the name of Christ 'the human form divine', because 'everything that lives is holy'. In its light Albert Schweitzer's doctrine of reverence for life is not as eccentric as orthodox believers have liked to suppose. It is the point of D. H. Lawrence's essay 'On Being Religious',[7] where it is put with such comic force that a long quotation will be welcome relief from theological wrangling.

The Great God has been treated to so many sighs, supplications, prayers, tears and yearnings that, for the time, He's had enough. There is, I believe, a great strike on in heaven. The Almighty has vacated the throne, abdicated, climbed down. It's no good your looking up into the sky. It's empty. Where the Most High used to sit listening to woes, supplications and repentances, there's nothing but a great gap in the empyrean. You can still go on praying to that gap, if you like. The Most High has gone out.

He has climbed down. He has just calmly stepped down the ladder of the angels, and is standing behind you. You can go on gazing and yearning up the shaft of hollow heaven if you like. The Most High just stands behind you, grinning to Himself.

Now this isn't a deliberate piece of blasphemy. It's just one way of stating an everlasting truth: or pair of truths. First, there is always the Great God. Second, as regards man, He shifts His position in the cosmos. The Great God departs from the heaven where man has located Him, and plumps His throne down somewhere else. Man, being an ass, keeps going to the same door to beg for his carrot, even when the Master has gone away to another house. The ass keeps on going to the same spring to drink, even when the spring has dried up, and there's nothing but clay and hoofmarks. It doesn't occur

to him to look round, to see where the water has broken out afresh, somewhere else out of some live rock. Habit! God has become a human habit, and Man expects the Almighty habitually to lend Himself to it. Whereas the Almighty – it's one of His characteristics – won't. He makes a move, and laughs when Man goes on praying to the gap in the Cosmos.
'Oh, little hole in the wall! Oh, little gap, holy little gap!' as the Russian peasants are supposed to have prayed, making a deity of the hole in the wall.
Which makes me laugh. And nobody will persuade me that the Lord Almighty doesn't roar with laughter, seeing all the Christians still rolling their imploring eyes to the skies where the hole is, which the Great God left when He picked up his throne and walked.

Another thing about criticism as an ally in the choosing necessary to faith: it is practical. Poring over a text, one of the gospels for example, the critic asks of it, in general and in detail, 'What is this for? What did it do or mean to achieve?' This is how the refusal to down tools on holy ground works out in practice. It is not a case of the abomination of desolation standing where he ought not, because religion in general, and Christianity in particular, is also a practical business meant to help people by being useful to them. It may be something more, more correctly it may be about something more, but if it is not *this* it does not matter. In finding out what a belief is good for, making the practical decision of whether it is worth the big choice of believing in it, the critic is not a nuisance but a desperately needed ally. Christianity requires that the doxological acclamation 'Glory to God in the highest' should be held together as tightly as possible with the critic's and the shopper's question 'what's it for?' Because only that way is the acclamation completed with '. . . and peace on earth to mankind in whom he delights'. That is a gnomic way of putting the question to be investigated in the next chapter.

2
Myths

❦

In 1950 a Papal Bull of Pius XII, *Munificentissimus Deus*, promulgated the dogma of the assumption into heaven of the Blessed Virgin Mary, united as Bride with God the Son in the heavenly bridechamber, united with the Godhead as the personification of wisdom (Sophia). It was an extraordinary performance for its date, and nothing quite like it may ever be seen again: one of the last achievements of the great old Roman dogma factory. In the climate of the mid-twentieth century the anachronism of it was breathtaking. There was no scientific historical evidence for such an event whatsoever; there were no objective discoveries of critical research to authenticate it. But the old dogma factory did not work to such specifications of authenticity. The assumption of Mary was believed in the piety of the faithful and pronounced as essential to faith by the authority, infallible in such matters, of the Pope. That was warrant enough. History, in such a context, is no problem. It is whatever authority says it is. To Protestant and rational minds this was, if not just toweringly silly, an act of provocative defiance against the disciplines in which they lived and by which they moved. The subjection of history to authority is to liberalism the most sinister possible threat to freedom.

But somebody, and he the son of a liberal Protestant pastor in Switzerland, was very pleased. Carl Gustav Jung in his *Answer to Job*, published only two years after *Munificentissimus Deus*, said: 'This dogma is in every respect timely, though very much to the astonishment of all

rationalists.'[1] He returned to it, impenitently, in his
autobiographical reminiscences of 1961:[2]

> The Christian nations have come to a sorry pass; their
> Christianity slumbers and has neglected to develop its myth
> further in the couse of the centuries. Those who gave
> expression to the dark stirrings of growth in mythic ideas
> were refused a hearing: Joachim of Flora, Meister Eckhart,
> Jacob Boehme, and many others have remained obscurantists
> for the majority. The only ray of light is Pius XII and his
> dogma. But people do not even know what I am referring to
> when I say this. They do not realise that a myth is dead if
> it no longer lives and grows. Our myth has become mute,
> and gives no answers. The fault lies not in it as it is set down
> in the Scriptures, but solely in us, who have not developed
> it further, who, rather, have suppressed any such attempts.
> The original version of the myth offers ample points of
> departure and possibilities of development.

Jung was teasing and being perfectly serious. As a child
he had gone to church and noticed a fatal contrast:
between the glowing gospel of God's goodness which his
father preached Sunday after Sunday, and the ever sad,
shut faces of his faithful hearers. The thing was not
working. The wheels of preaching went round and round
in majestic circularity – and geared into nothing, made
nothing.

The rationalists, of whom Jung is so briskly dismissive,
had not been idle. Biblical criticism, in its momentous
modern scientific phase, had been well under way for a
century when Jung was a boy. The examination of biblical
books on the dissecting tables of criticism had produced
plenty of results in the line of historical anatomizing, and
they formed part of a Protestant pastor's training. In fact,
Jung owed a lot to it because it had done as much as
classical scholarship, if not more, to pin-point the category
of myth, insofar as such a vast and ramifying thing can
be pigeon-holed, and so make it available for conscious
discussion and use.[3] It had been objectified: and so, as
well as being made available, put at a certain distance
from people who were conscious of it and made it into
something which they were free consciously to criticize or
use. Jung could not have done without that, nor could the

psycho-analytical movement as a whole, and it was a debt to the rational-analytical mind which makes Jung's dismissiveness unjust. But the freedom got by critical analysis had been spent, not so much in creative use and development, as in yet more analysing. There Jung was more than just; he was being a good physician and therapist. The wasting disease of the church was its fear of imaginative development of myths. The talent, which should have been exhibited on the open market, it kept wrapped up. Others set to and developed the myths creatively – many more than Jung's trio of mystics. There was William Blake, whose anti-rationalism would have endeared him to Jung as much as his energetic myth-making. There were Hölderlin and Goethe. There were still more who knew about the first achievements of biblical criticism, positively accepted them and from that point went on to make and create: Wagner, the admirer of Strauss, in Germany, and in England, Coleridge with *The Ancient Mariner* and *Kubla Khan*; George Eliot in *Middlemarch* and *Daniel Deronda*; Browning exploring the marriage of ideal vision with history in the mind of John the Evangelist in *A Death in the Desert*.[4] However much these names mean to odd individuals within the church, they have not been officially applauded by the authorities who represent the church at large or claimed by them on its behalf. Mainstream Christian spirituality and worship go along without them and, compared with the techniques of criticism, they play practically no part in the training of theologians. They are left to 'literature'.

As a physician Jung recognized this state of mainstream Christianity as a disease, a state of psychic arrest such as he had discovered in so many patients paralysed by fear of adventure into the unknown. One of them had been a theologian.

> He had a certain dream which was frequently repeated. He dreamt that he was standing on a slope from which he had a beautiful view of a low valley covered with dense woods. In the dream he knew that in the middle of the woods there was a lake, and he also knew that hitherto something had always prevented him from going there. But this time he

wanted to carry out his plan. As he approached the lake, the atmosphere grew uncanny, and suddenly a light gust of wind passed over the surface of the water, which rippled darkly. He awoke with a cry of terror.[5]

After dream or vision comes critical analysis, after that the possibility of creative freedom – a succession which is the key to this whole discussion. Jung was surprised that the theologian did not recognize images in the dream which were part of his professional stock-in-trade. The wind is the creator spirit in the Bible. It 'troubles the waters' in the miracle at the pool of Bethesda in John 5 as a prelude to the healing of paralysis: which is itself (a development Jung missed) a new version of the creative spirit-wind moving over the face of the waters at Genesis 1.2. Not only did the theologian miss the connections, he refused to make them. 'All very well,' says Jung scathingly, 'to speak of the Holy Spirit on occasions – but it is not a phenomenon to be experienced!' A paragraph later he is gentler. Most people run from the surfacing of inner experiences, and 'theologians are in a more difficult situation than others. On the one hand they are closer to religion, but on the other hand they are more bound by church and dogma.' There is the problem. His diagnosis remains. And who is going to man-handle paralysed theology, with its myths atrophied because they are criticized but not made anew, into the troubled waters where it could come to walk again? It must be done, and something much more than Pentecostalism in its usual English versions is needed because that, after freaking out, relapses into the restrictive rigidities of conservative respectability. It must be done because myths, like us, come to partings of the ways. They get better or worse, are capable of lucid conversations with others or go off their heads into fugal monologues, develop or die.

As a prelude to therapy, some analysis is always necessary. How, in point of historical fact, has Christianity come to Jung's 'sorry pass'? To get a clearer idea of the force of his strictures and a glimpse of a cure, a long and complicated story in intellectual history must be made short and simple.

We all, including Jung, owe too much to the Protestant intellectual tradition to approach it in a slighting spirit. It is distinguished by its independent-minded attention to facts and its brilliant development of the power of analysis in freedom from any dogmatic authority. The Reformation dealt an analytically reductionist blow to that old dominion by its principle of *sola scriptura*. 'The Bible, and the Bible only, is the religion of Protestants,' said Chillingworth. And his tone of voice was negative, reductionist, opposed to the authoritative accretions of the Roman church. It is some measure of the seriousness of our present situation that now that slogan of his, much faded, is flown over the beleaguered citadel of conservatively biblical, including fundamentalist, Christianity. Then it was the battle cry of a brave dash into the open. The old moribund religion, together with the myths and legends it cultivated to make history subserve its dogma and fit into it, was left behind. A ring had been broken, the primal nugget restored. Bunyan's Christian ran out of the doomed city, a solitary individual with a book in his hand and miles to go before he slept. That book is the key. It was God's pure and primal word. Unlike the catholic trappings, he was its author. Institutionalized Protestantism in England was told that in the golden and godly days of 'the ancient fathers' the whole Bible had been read in church every year, whereas in more recent and darker times this decent order had been 'broken and neglected, by planting in uncertain stories and legends'. Dethroning an authority involves first, the labelling of its myths as such; second, the discarding of them as unnecessary. The spirit, and the threat, of the Reformation is similar to that of the 1977 myth *furore* and continuous with it (see p. 17 below). Analysis, rational distinction, was the way out of the labyrinthine nightmare of mystery and authority. It was a principle that was to make any kind of institutionalized religion, including Protestantism, insecure ever after. The radical heyday of mid-seventeenth-century England made that clear. Men thought for themselves and came up with ideas about the Bible, authority and the nature of Christ, so startlingly fresh that they still upset the ecclesiastical authorities when radical theologians hit on them again in our day. Order was broken up by the eruptions. It was too much, and in the end made the restoration of Charles II welcome. The pilgrims had to get on their way again with the book in their hands – many from Norwich and the countryside around it across the Atlantic to New England.

The conjunction (in the name of freedom) of the acid of reductionist analysis with the *sola scriptura* principle was a time bomb. It could not be long before the one ate through into the other and blew the myth of the book's authority itself sky-high. The first notable explosion was Lessing's publication of Reimarus' *Fragments* in 1774-8, the second and more resounding, Strauss's *Life of Jesus* in 1835. The message was as clear as it was dreadful. 'Uncertain stories and legends' were not confined to silly apocryphal books or benighted anthologies like *The Golden Legend*. They were in the very pages of the Bible itself, and even in the gospels. So the figure of Jesus Christ, which is centrally authoritative in Christianity as God's pure word and deed revealed – *this* was seen to be mixed up with them, so intricately as to be, as it proved, inextricable. The shock of certainties revealed to be uncertain, of hard historical facts to be figments of (however keen-eyed or inspired) imagination, has not been absorbed yet. In England in 1977 there was a furore about the book of (mainly academic) essays called *The Myth of God Incarnate*. Christian people did not even need to read the book to be upset. The title was objectionable enough because it labelled as 'myth' a central and integral Christian doctrine, and in ordinary speech myth is a dismissive word which knocks anything it hits into the dustbin of discarded dreams. But this ordinary sense of myth is too narrow and too impatient to do full justice to something very broad and apparently indispensable to full human living. Academics, whatever else may be said of them, are more patient with some ordinary things than ordinary people: with myths as with light, history or language. Among them the word means something else and more. It is not rubbish, but sacred tales which give shape to religious mystery, 'the expression of unobservable realities in terms of observable phenomena'.[6] It is the work of poets, makers, whose eyes,

> glance from heaven to earth, from earth to heaven;
> And, as imagination bodies forth
> The form of things unknown, the poet's pen
> Turns them to shapes, and gives to airy nothing
> A local habitation and a name.[7]

Here the poets agree with people who are popularly supposed to be more practical, sociologists and anthropologists, as well as with theologians. Myths are, in fact, practical achievements. They objectify forces which are at work anyhow, by giving them the names and places which make up stories. So they put at arm's length what was chaotically undifferentiated from us before, and that helps us to cope with it. We are relieved as when the doctor gives a name to a shapeless pain dominating our bodies (and so our minds), or a counsellor diagnoses a discomfort agitating and lowering our spirits (and so our bodies). It is not a cure or a final resolution, but it suggests the possibility of one, and meanwhile is a practical help.

It is not exactly a cure or a final resolution. That is important. Some writers about myth, such as Lévi-Strauss, put this so strongly as to say that myths combine opposites which never can be resolved. They mix gods, men, animals, trees and rivers into hybrids: centaurs, dryads, the minotaur, angels, divine incarnations in people or beasts or rivers. They are about the impossible. This is obviously offensive to religious people who have myths which, they believe, save them and integrate them: myths that have happened and work. It is less offensive to religious people of a different, and rarer, kind. For them the force of religion consists in clearly facing the opposite as opposite: death as death and not a gateway to life, God as God and not a very (ultimately) important man or person. Don Cupitt stands for this majestic tradition, in all its stern purity, in his outright attacks on incarnation.[8] God is in heaven and you are on earth, therefore let your words be few – and your myths of hybrid incarnation fewer still.

But are these flights of fancy so dispensable? History repeats itself. That is often said. And often denied because in the inexorable passage of time the past is past and never comes back – an important point morally as well as scientifically. Yet there is something valuable in saying that history repeats itself. It points to similar patterns in human goings on which are separated from one another by large tracts of time and cultural space, patterns which are likely to be repeated and so pragmatically worth knowing about. There is moral point here, too, making historical study into something more than a purely scientific exercise (if there is such a thing); into something which matters beyond the archives and the seminar room. This opens history to the imaginative realm where it may connect with the myths which do much to keep historians at their arduous tasks: Old Testament historians believing in a divine plan, Greek or modern Marxist ones believing in certain energetic constants of human nature and destiny. But a price is paid for such achievements of relevance. The necessary abstracted patterns which do it will always distort perception of the facts in some measure; and the only corrective is to let the facts have another say, marshalling them in a way meant to make dents or cracks in the pattern – since they can never be marshalled to no purpose or 'purely' objectively. The aim is the establishment of a new imaginative pattern or the revision of the old one, and usually a bit of both. So history is a continual argument between divisive analysis and unifying imaginative pattern-making: not just in the study of it when it has happened, but also in the making of it while it is going on.

Myths need frequent analytical servicing, but that is not to say that they are just about the impossible and the improper. They are hybrids because opposite things do overlap. Gods, men, animals and trees share a world and so are together and interact. Time present and time past flow into one another and out of them, ominously, flows the future which we are always worrying about. Myths describe the interactions: natural ones those between apparently constant beings such as animals and men, historical ones those between changing things such as epochs of history, and offering aetiological ('how did it

come to be so?') and apocalyptic ('what will become of it?')
stories to do so. Such pattern-stories look on the surface
like things which happened once and just as they say –
or will. Underneath, they describe things which happen
over and over again roughly, but never exactly, as they
say.

What happens if this more positive way of looking at
myths is applied to the incarnation of God in Jesus Christ?
The orthodox Christian reader is likely to feel a little relief
and rather more foreboding at the prospect. It promises
to take his belief in the incarnation seriously by appreciating
that it is genuinely about something. But it also promises
to make that 'something' much less tidy and defined than
he has been led to think it is, much less immune from
aggressive criticism. Incarnation is usually confined by him
to the historical and divine figure of Jesus as its unique
instance. Yet that is not at all as simple and definite as
it looks. A historical human life is a complicated and
ramifying thing, always moving and always in connection
and relation with other lives, and adding divinity to the
mixture does not exactly make it more confined. Even if
divine incarnation is confined to Jesus, there is a whole
life to consider: not just a birth which introduces him into
the checkable complexities of society, but a growing into
them too; a long story of suffering and doing, arguing and
agreeing, facing death and dying, and something beyond
death. Even such a sketchy recitation of what is entailed
in a human life is enough to show that it is never isolated,
and brings to mind the famous quotation from John Donne
that 'no man is an island entire of itself but a part of the
continent and the main'. So even the devout eye which
contemplates Jesus as the divine incarnation in a human
life cannot rest there; because if an incarnation in the long
chain of history is as seriously meant as it seems to be,
vital connection with antecedents and consequences is
involved. The tree has roots and branches as well as a
trunk. The prophets of the Old Testament, even the whole
Old Testament itself, have been seen from the first
beginnings of Christianity as 'foretelling' Christ. It is no
longer possible, as then and in mediaeval stained glass

windows, to see this as a collection of lucky (inspired) forecasts not related to their own time but only to a time to come. We have learned to take history more seriously than that, to see an event in past time more in its own colours and less in those of another time. The Old Testament writers meant something then, in their present related to past and future. They were not so much busy with crystal balls as with the interaction of transcendent God with the developing scene of their day, the only crystal ball they had; in deeds and sufferings as well as words which 'glance from heaven to earth, from earth to heaven'. This is a more thorough and concrete fore-telling of the incarnation than we get from the reading of snippets of prophecy at carol services – and more real in itself. Not only are Jesus' predecessors involved in any myth or doctrine about him. His followers are, too, and this is integral to the beginnings of Christianity. The myths and doctrines about him are there for people to make their own in active obedience and not just for assent or admiration. They are to be made incarnate again in the lives of other sons and daughters of God. They are thoroughly social.

Enough has already been said to fulfil the forebodings of untidiness and lack of definite limits – and the discussion has been confined to the Bible interpreted in a traditional enough way. This was not enough in the early church. It lived in a world dominated by Greek religion and philosophy. These had already infiltrated some of the biblical books, and they nourished and inspired many of the best Christian minds. So Plato and Socrates were acknowledged as having a connection, usually presented in a legendary way, with Christian truth. And so it has gone on and on, developing in the way Jung applauded as necessary to being alive, up to our own worried religious present. But we have to admit that there has been a cost. A hymn speaks of the divine action in Christ as 'once, only once, and once for all'. It is, as usual in orthodox pronouncements, a nice balance. In a narrowly objective historical view it is obviously true that Jesus died once and only once, but there is no religious nourishment in simply saying so. The religious point of 'once, only once' is, first and positively, to ground theology in a point in concrete history; second and negatively, to stop it spilling into any more points in concrete history. The control of this second and negative point is valuable to religious order but potentially stultifying to religious life. St Paul believed the death of Christ to be something happening in himself and his fellow Christians in as historically concrete a way as ever it was: in the horrors of travel, the grind of church administration, the rites of baptism. The hymn tries to cope with this by the counter-balance of 'once for all', but it would be more loyal to Paul to say 'over and over again in all', who 'bear about in their bodies the dying of the Lord Jesus'. In an obvious and almost literal sense, the future of the doctrine lies more in the second point (positive and inclusive) than the first with its exclusive emphasis, because it is about something for us to experience historically. Orthodoxy, with the privilege of abstraction, balances opposites between which discipleship has to choose when it gets down to them. The choice will be temporary, as ever, but is necessary to intelligibility – in discipleship and not just the life of the mind. And in terms of discipleship the choice here of 'for all' is practically mandatory. In terms of history, too, the exclusive principle is made shaky by the impossibility of isolating historical events in a final, hard-and-fast way.

Some such parting of the ways is inevitable. For too long, and now too often, defenders of Christianity have tried to have their cake of historical religion and eat it. The 1978 BBC Reith Lectures were again a case in point. Edward Norman applied his historian's sense of the socially and historically conditioned nature of Christianity over a vast range and wittily. But when he came to Christ in the final lecture the tone and method changed completely. The tense emotional appeal of the pulpit took over from the relaxed quizzicality of the study. The continual insistence on the entanglement of sacred and secular in history stopped and the categories 'unique' and 'revelation' came in to describe a Christ who was *the* exception to everything else that had been discussed because he alone spoke and represented unconditioned eternal truth. This is theology working by hiatus, calling off the dogs of criticism at the crucial point. It is not uncommon in more subdued forms amongst New Testament scholars, who use a theological version of an economic 'stop-go' policy. They sometimes treat their scriptural material analytically and critically, but more mildly than similar material of similar date. There is a touch on the brakes. In dealing with a miracle story in a canonical gospel, attention may be diverted from the wild improbability of the thing by scrupulous attention to its symbolism, source, or christology. By contrast, with a miracle from elsewhere (*The Acts of Peter*, say) the improbability is paraded and the other things scarcely glimpsed. It is a throwing of stones at other people's glass houses as old as the first Christian apologists at least. In its present, more subdued, form, however, the mildness is veiled in the scrupulous intricacy of New Testament criticism. There is, perhaps, no more exacting discipline. But it is caught between a conscious awareness of myths and a conscious awareness of facts and the difference between the two, and this is so worrying, so sharp a dilemma, that there is a natural tendency to oscillate between its points rather than to get on and get out. How, indeed, are we honestly to get on and get out? There can be no going back to the dreaming innocence of pre-critical days. We have eaten the fruit which opens our eyes to differences we didn't recognize before. We are outside Eden with the spade of criticism in our hands. We dig away energetically until we get to the centre of Christianity, and there we pause.

At this point another method is likely to take over. Into the hiatus comes a forgetting of the known differences. It speaks in remarks under the grand heading of 'our historic faith' which begin with the words 'the fact of . . . ' – 'the fact of the incarnation', 'the fact of the resurrection', 'the fact of the contemporary and living Christ'. A lot of this sort of thing greeted Bultmann's great airing of the question of myth.[9] Central things of Christianity are being spoken of here, but the use of the word 'fact' has more bravado to it than aptness. It is half-true at best, for these are all things where, for all their religious centrality, fact and imagination are mixed in various proportions. This conservative reaction disqualifies itself by its great reluctance to grow up into the awareness we have of differences and the job of sorting them out. The confusion inherent in it is seen in the way in which it often pays homage to the scientific point of view in its crasser forms by making fact the ultimate court of appeal. Because whatever-it-is is a fact it is authoritative – all but forgetting that imagination is integral to science and that an indispensable part of the authority of religious statements is in their appeal to the imagination. In this way it is religiously inadequate, because it stops the wheels gearing in.

Yet another attempt at resolution works by using our awareness of difference and pointing out that the incarnation, the resurrection, the presence of Christ, are mythical truths: with historical grounding, usually of a complex sort, but mythical for all that. This is the radical or modernist reaction which, while it insists, again with a measure of bravado, on historically being its age yet, by its correct analytical labelling, brings down the temperature drastically. And temperature is very important in religion. To believe that certain things did not really happen is very different from believing that they did – a thinner sort of diet. This was Strauss's trouble. He thought that he was delivering the church from the banal special pleading of rationalist biblical interpreters with their fact-orientation (Jesus had a store of bread in a cave behind him, was just paddling at the edge of the lake, and so on) into the glorious world of imaginative meaning – and so giving it back its life-blood. To a devotee of Mozart's *The Magic Flute* (he used to sing 'O Isis and Osiris' in the bath) this made splendid sense. The church thought otherwise. It is just not the same to believe, for example, that incarnation is a more or less apt way to think about Jesus at a particular time as to believe that he was God incarnate as a matter of hard, unassailable fact. Meaning without deed is inadequate in religion as it is in ethics. So still the wheels, though academically clean and decent, don't gear in. It is not enough to mean and to dream even when we have the great advantage of knowing that that is what we are doing. We want to know what is concretely possible, not only what has happened but also what could happen.

So what is to be done? The old-timers are in a tangle. Their conservatism is usually, in fact, the modernism of fifty years ago, for example on the first chapters of Genesis, taken up without acknowledgement of previous hostility to it.[10] They invite us to live religiously in yesterday's world. The modernists are clear and live in and for today's world, getting the labels right for the time being. But if the time being is to be adequately served in religion there must be, taking up Jung's point, development and making of myths as well as analysis of them. Without that, 'modernism' is itself a misleading term because too much of its time and energy goes into raking over, albeit with very refined and precise rakes, the past. And it attracts the resentment of many sensitive spirits as well as that of the backwoodsmen:

> Our meddling intellect
> Misshapes the beauteous form of things;
> – we murder to dissect.

It, too, can be philistine.

It will be a long journey to get an answer to the question of what's to be done. But long journeys, in the Chinese proverb, begin with a single step. The single step for now is to see something of the practical, even political interaction of myths and facts, dreamers and analysts, and two examples from this century will get it under way.

The first is the myth of Nazism as presented by Goebbels in 1936:

> When the Führer addressed his last appeal to us on March 28, it was as if a profound agitation went through the whole nation; one felt that Germany was transformed into one single House of God, in which its intercessor stood before the throne of the Almighty to bear witness . . . it seemed to us that this cry to heaven of a people for freedom and peace could not die away unheard. This was religion in its profoundest and most mystical sense. A nation then acknowledged God through

its spokesman, and laid its destiny and its life with full confidence in his hand.

The second comes from the Civil Rights movement in America. In his 1963 speech at the Lincoln Memorial in Washington, Martin Luther King said:

> I have a dream that the sons of former slaves and the sons of former slave owners will be able to sit together at the table of brotherhood (*crowd*: Yes! Yes! I see it!). I have a dream that my four little children will one day live in a nation where they will not be judged by the colour of their skin but by the content of their character (*crowd*: Oh, yes! Dream on! Dream!).

Are they both myths? Goebbels' is so much more high-flown than King's that it seems to play it out of the court of myth. The intercessor standing before the throne is bigger stuff than the people sitting round the table. But both get their force from the simultaneous appeal of apt historical timing with prophetic vision. Goebbels' looks impossible because it is more abstract and grand, but it was meant to be made historically actual – and in some dreadful measure was. King's looks possible because it is more domestic, but will the day when race does not matter ever come? He meant it to, and worked for it to, but there is still aptness in the crowd's 'dream on!' They are both myths in the sense that, within a wide use of the term, they hitch the wagon of society to an imagined star. Things will not turn out exactly as either of them says, but something like it, something of the vision, will turn out if the myth catches on in history. Germany, or most of it, did lay its destiny in Hitler's hands. Black and white have sat at table together. But in neither case is the matter closed.

The power of imaginative vision is made very clear by these quotations and their momentous contexts. Our own times must be included in the contexts because we are still living with their fall-out. The decision for or against a myth, whether to jump on it and be carried along or say 'no' and keep clear, is nothing less than the decision of faith which has irrevocable consequences in action. Myths, as perceptions of what is not yet fully done, get things done. They move mountains, historically and politically, because they are integral to faith. Faith and myth go together and work over the same territory. Myth is the form of imagination which connects the deep things of human consciousness to other deep things which are beyond it and greater: the future, the land, the nation, or God. It holds together the age-old poles of religion, the immanent (what is right inside us and our world) and the transcendent (what eludes us so that we can't get ourselves right round it). It arouses the nameless and faceless forces within to move and to disturb: even to get names and faces, for myth is itself a sort of analysis. It gives us glimpses of things to aim at, destructively or constructively, because they are at present beyond our grasp. So they give off energy. Faith has the same pattern. It is the movement of imagination in which a person in his or her deepest self connects to something greater which he cannot entirely apprehend and dominate but can aim at – to realize it or to break it up. It is hard to imagine a faith without a myth or a myth without a faith. The myth may be soberly dressed in the abstract nouns which philosophers prefer to the knockabout characters of the apocalyptists, in sober realism or glittering fancy-dress, but it will still be there, waiting for the assent or dissent of faith – in other words, for commitment or rejection. It only has to be clear and intelligible enough to make that choice possible. The question then is how to choose, on what grounds to say yes or no.

To say that we have a choice in the face of myths is perhaps as big and risky an expression of belief in free will as one could make. Do not myths, after all, mould us and push us about? They have a lot to do with those unspoken and unconscious forces in any age which T. E. Hulme called 'doctrines felt as facts',[11] all the more determinative for being taken for granted, a sort of invisible juggernauts. Don't they determine us? Yes. Certainly yes for most of the people most of the time, because they have not objectified them or acknowledged any distancing distinction. The very subjectivity of their belief gives it its power.[12] They feel them as facts. But not for all the people all the time. There have been Galileo and Einstein, Jesus and Voltaire and others who did not, as an unconscious reflex, bow the knee to the assumptions of the day, who were historical instances, or incarnations of the archetypal little boy in Hans Christian Andersen's fairy story of the Emperor's New Clothes. We can even measure time by them (the age of Voltaire, before Einstein and after, BC and AD) because of the decisive changes they made in what we take for granted. They somehow got hold of a lever which moved the world – meaning our description and understanding of the world, because we do not live in a place but in a description of a place. They were children of their time, having predecessors to whom they owed large debts. Yet they got themselves that little but vital distance from the notions then currently believed in. That bit of space and chink of detachment was as essential to their creativity as the space between the painter and his canvas. Most important of all for our subject, such a little jump of discontinuity had big consequences because it enabled them to look afresh at, and relativize, the cohesive myths that were current, so that the myths' hold on them was loosened. To such people the myth, which is so subjective to other people that they are not aware of it as such, was objectified: something they could weigh up and assess from a distance. It often followed that they were put down as blasphemers, subverters of order and obscurantists. And there was something in such charges because relativity allows freedom and freedom allows relativizing (which comes first?), and the symptoms of it are social giddiness and agoraphobia. But how did they do it? That question leads a good way into the big question of what we are to do.

First, they won that detachment by a leap of reason – not from reason, but of reason. The Nazi myth of race was based on 'scientific' research into race which was scientifically demonstrably bogus. Blessed were those who did their analytical homework, found it to be so, and stepped aside. Reason is vital because spiritual nose and gut reaction on their own can be so cruelly and easily deceived. Nazism had a good smell of biblical theology

(Goebbels in that speech seems to owe something to the Epistle to the Hebrews) and the big outdoors. It beguiled some members of the English upper classes, including the odd church-leader. Critical analysis was needed, and even those who could not make scientific checks on the Nazi mythology could lay Goebbels' vision of a free and consecrated nation against the everyday facts of religious persecution on the streets and in the camps. Reason, working by the detached analysis of facts, gave distance and room for the evaluation of a myth. By relativizing, it gave the saving possibility of escape from falsehood and, in old-time religious terminology, from damnation. The good thing about Martin Luther King's myth, by contrast, is its modest reasonableness. He has been up the mountain of vision but, instead of the grand scene of mystical dedication which Goebbels witnessed, he saw from there something almost banal in its reasonableness and possibility: people having a meal together and getting acquainted.

But if reason is indispensable, still it is not enough. For all its realism and down-to-earth possibility, King's vision was still of a future not yet attained and so called for a loyalty of faith. If we look at the Germans who said no to Nazism, we find that as well as a capacity for analysis (and some of them had only a saving little of that), they had an alternative myth. For Bonhoeffer it was Christianity and, within that over-capacious term, a Christianity indebted to Karl Barth in its distrust of natural theology. He changed later in prison, but that gave him the lever then, at the point of saying no to the Third Reich. For von Stauffenberg and others it was aristocratic military honour. For many others it was Marxism. For Franz Jägerstetter, the Austrian sexton, it was his Catholic penny catechism.

Reason and allegiance to another myth: these together gave the possibility of getting that little bit of freedom which, though under pressure from all sides by whatever is determined and unfree, makes all the difference. The freedom may often be no more than the minimal kind of a free assent to, or grasping of, that which is determined. Bonhoeffer did this by deliberately returning from America to Germany in 1939. Hamlet seems never quite to have got round to doing it. Relativizing is a built-in part of this conjunction of freedom and myth which is so much to the advantage of them both. That is to say something which is very surprising to traditional religious people, as to traditional Marxists. They complain that relativizing is a death-threat. It is exactly that to a religion or a political ideology which works by total submission to authoritative myth felt as fact – to religion and ideology as usually established. But is this the only possible kind of ideology religion, more particularly, of Christianity? Very likely not. And in saying 'very likely not' one is not only gazing into a crystal ball to see the outlines of a Christianity which might be, but also referring to kinds of Christianity which already exist. Under the credal banners, under the great lid of traditional orthodoxy, there are plenty of Christians who do not make the total submission of a *sacrificium intellectus* (or, intellectual suicide) and do not intend to. And they are not confined to universities. Confronted with the apparent demand for total submission to myths in which they find no nutritional or liberating value, they tend to keep quiet, while holding on to the articles of the creed in which they do find such value, or slip out. Yet their ways can be articulated as kinds of Christianity – and Christianity always comes, in practice, in kinds. However partially, compared with the range of orthodox tradition, they work out the conjunction of religious symbols with secular life which Christianity demands, not least in the heart of the myth of incarnation itself. Such Christianity will obviously be far from monolithic. It will be in a phase of experiments conducted by individuals or small informal groups and networks of them – the big formal groups (churches) have an obligation to stock the full traditional range. In relation to comprehensive credal statements, they are something like allied underground movements, more or less on their side, not entirely under their control but hopefully under their blessing. They could (and do) plead as a precedent the churches of the New Testament, producing their own indigenous versions of the gospel, each with its achievements and shortcomings, before the full-scale creeds were invented.[13] Nowadays they are likely

to be more aware of the temporary and exploratory
character of their work than then. This is the cross that
they have to carry – the sense of their own relativity. But
if this can be seen as integral to the Christian doctrine of
Christ, because it also belongs to him as a human being
set in historical relativities, and because it is saving of
humanity, it cannot be denied that they are integrally
Christian. Totally Christian they are not, but that belongs
to no individual or group, and only to the entirety of a
whole tradition bigger than any of them, to which they
can contribute only in their way.

Conclusion

Is a myth done for once it has been spotted and
acknowledged as myth? Does it then lose its saving power
for people? The fanatic gives a loudly silent no by refusing
the labelling and charging ahead in the undiminished zeal
of his subjectivity. The more enlightened person who
accepts it slows down – they would say, to a halt. Or he
moves into a bleaker and more sophisticated world of lost
innocence, toiling away in the sweat of his brow. According
to one writer he is a cuckoo in the nest of believers.[14]
Perhaps a runt in the litter would be an apter metaphor.

> Oh I know we must put away the beautiful stories
> And learn to be good in a dull way without enchantment,
> Yes, we must.[15]

Yet it is not quite as bad or simple as that. Goodness,
though hard work, is never exactly dull and always a little
amazing. And enchantment comes in at least two kinds:
the total because subjectively unconscious, and the modified
because conscious. There is enchantment which survives
critical knowledge of the enchanter and is better for it.
People who attend enthusiastically to Wagner's modern
myth of power and redeeming love-death, *The Ring*, or to
Tolkien's less convincing effort, do not have the least doubt
that it is a myth that they are attending to; and still they
get moral and spiritual help from it. In an age which
knows better than ever before the vast range of religious
experience and myths, idolatrous positivism is out of court.

The total Wagnerite is as much an anachronistic 'last survivor of the age of chivalry' as the totally orthodox Christian. By the same token an exclusive or uncritical marriage to the spirit of the age has little future.

An example may serve to show the positive value of the modification of enchantment by consciousness. The doctrine of Christ's sinlessness has, for many people, given trouble to the point of getting unproductively stuck. A little analysis could get it moving again, though in a rather different way. The root of the trouble comes from dealing with the doctrine with tools got only from the pragmatic historian's workshop. These, if not exactly the wrong tools, are inadequate to the job, because more than narrow historical inquiry is at stake here. Was Jesus, in point of historical fact, sinless? To say that it is unlikely is not to deny it, but suggests that historically it is not thinkable. The historian, as historian, will walk away from it with a verdict of *non liquet*. It cannot be made to stick within his terms of reference and so, strictly and narrowly as a historian, he cannot be interested in it. He may well think it unlikely because Jesus was not like the old man of Hong Kong who never did anything wrong because he lay on his back with his head in a sack, but was on the contrary a public man faced by choices between evils and inevitably doing harm (e.g. Judas) in the train of doing good. The difficulty rubs off on the believer who, if he too leaves it in these terms, will probably also walk away from it. How can a sinless Christ possibly be made to look realistic? And there is another and consequent problem. The believer is not just looking for a plausible 'photographic' historical realism. He is looking for realism about human nature in his image of Christ, and here too sinlessness is very hard to sort with a state of affairs to which, as he knows it, faults and shortcomings are integral. In the doctrine of salvation the unassumed is the unhealed, and this makes sinlessness a problem which does not go away when the force of (unsuccessful) temptation is invoked. We still have to cope with sin as part of our nature and not just an external pressure on it.

I have been careful to talk in terms of difficulty rather

than denial and hope that the reader will give me credit for it, because it is important for the next step and not just for ecclesiastical self-defence. The next step is to wonder about tools and method. We have been jumping, rather desperately, from the abstractions of doctrinal assertion to the concrete realism of history and back again. But between these two lies myth, semi-abstract and semi-concrete, as a vital connection which we have ignored to our confusion. In myth we do not have either pure ideas or realistically fully-drawn characters but something between the two. In particular, myth presents us with *dramatis personae* who each stand for an aspect of human nature to the exclusion of others. It is something like a 'comedy of humours'. Human nature is not with one of the *personae* but with all of them and their interaction. One *persona* will stand for the light, another for the dark within us, and so on, representing analytically or diagnostically a force within the more complex organism which is our historical business. So in *The Ring* the hero Siegfried 'bodies forth' conquering light by his fearlessness. This, again, presents an insoluble problem in realistic presentation which singers and producers knock their heads against. He is something of a vexatious liability as a character on stage – until he is brought up against the other hero, Hagen, who bodies forth engulfing darkness. Then we see the point. Siegfried is the white hope who encounters and absorbs Hagen's deadly melancholy. He is light only in order to be forced against the darkness. And though engulfed by it, he posthumously triumphs and reconciliation is accomplished through the clash. Both heroes are baffling in terms of realistic 'outscape', because they belong to the human 'inscape' of myth and make sense in its terms and not the other's.

It is beginning to be obvious that the doctrine of Christ's sinlessness can be restored to religious sense in the same terms. Nor do they have to be imposed. They are inherent in the two New Testament texts where the doctrine is most clearly stated. At I Corinthians 5.21 Paul explains the reconciliation of man and God in Christ, seeing Christ not realistically as a particular sort of human character but as

the bearer of divinity. 'For our sake God made him to be
sin who knew no sin, so that in him we might become
the righteousness of God.' And, lest there should be any
mistake about the sort of serious language-game that is
being played, all is set under the rubric or stage-direction
'even though we once regarded Christ according to the
flesh (i.e. from the standpoint of outward, historical reality
or realism as "merely human"), we regard him thus no
longer' (verse 16). Christ as an inward spiritual force is
the light which, in a momentous interchange, absorbs the
darkness and triumphs over it in reconciliation. That is
what his sinlessness is for. In the Epistle to the Hebrews
myth is on its home ground of ritual. Jesus is a 'great high
priest'. It is, at first sight and from the standpoint of
historical realism, a startlingly incongruous role for so anti-
clerical a historical figure who was over against the high
priest of his day, and was condemned and disowned by
him. But that is the wrong standpoint. In ritual, and the
myths which explain it, the eternal and inward work of
priesthood is the reconciliation of man and God. In this
context Jesus is to the Christian writer the priest of priests.
He is like us, but unlike us – again, a *persona* embodying
one of the eternal forces which meet in us, not a
realistically drawn character. 'For we have not a high priest
who is unable to sympathize with our weaknesses, but
one who in every respect has been tempted like as we are,
yet without sinning' (4.15). The sacrificial priest, like the
sacrificial victim, had to be spotlessly pure as well as
integrally human in order fully to absorb and neutralize
the opposite, the defilement of sin. Only so can reconciliation be fully achieved. The writer capitalizes on pointing
out that these stringent conditions have not been met
before. Now they are, by Christ: as priest and victim, like
us – and unlike us in one essential respect. But when and
where is that 'now'? The moment of Christ's death on the
cross. But, and this is all-important, that place and moment
are seen so inwardly as a spiritual action in heaven that
they become eternal. Christ is not a reconciling high priest
for one moment only, but priest and victim combined in
an imaginative *coup* transcending history and for ever.

The example has been sketchily treated and the thought of the writer of Hebrews is so complex that it is hard to do him detailed justice. But whatever qualifications of detail may be made, the main point stands. The doctrine of Christ's sinlessness, as a part of the Christian gospel of salvation, cannot be got to work without its mythical context. Otherwise it is a fish out of water. To try to prove or imagine it exclusively by standards of materialist historical realism is futile and baffling. To apprehend it in its spiritual inwardness is to get hold of something extremely valuable and useful. It is, in a full religious sense, a blessing to know what is going on and so how to approach and appreciate it.

Believers are being called to something trickier and more interesting than the outright championing or rejection of myths, or the entirely detached analysis of them, if that is possible. They are being called to evaluate and use them sensibly, whether they are their own or other people's, in the cause of human goodness which they believe to be God's cause. In the dynamic pattern of the doctrinal myth of incarnation, the cause of love draws the visionary figure down from the unassailable throne to be with us as an instructive helper for our hearts and heads.

The downward movement, into the world of historical relativity, makes universally saving the myths which would otherwise be restrictively enslaving. It saves us from the demonic treadmill of being lived by powers we do not understand. And it does so by a double movement. First it liberates and enlightens by making myths objectively accessible so that we have the freedom to size them up. Second, in asking the critic's question 'what is this myth for?', it delivers from the moral vertigo induced by the acknowledgement of relativity on its own: a vertigo which, if not cured, induces either desperate bravado or cynicism. It delivers from this by indicating a moral goal, a point to fix the mind's eye on and so steady oneself by moving towards it. Without that we are like the man in the parable who tidies up his house but, finding the result boring and vacuous, falls prey to worse chaos. In the Christian context the question 'what is this myth for?' asks 'how does it bring us nearer to other people and God?'

It brings us nearer to other people if it promotes brotherhood. The statement is not as tautologous as it sounds because its intention is to exclude our relating to other people as tyrants to be kow-towed to or as lesser beings to be used, even if they would prefer it that way. This kind of love, the famous Christian *agape*, is only possible to those for whom other people with their virtues and faults are as interesting as themselves, with theirs. And because everyone demands 'love me, love the myth I live for!', it is only possible to those for whom other people's myths, with their virtues and shortcomings, are as interesting as theirs – with theirs. The word 'interesting' is used deliberately because it balances the detachment and attachment which are both necessary to love. And it wards off something which is often mistaken for love but works against it: obsession. Since loving anybody consists largely in helping them to live without obsession, it can only be done by those who have been liberated from it in some measure, and then only in that measure. 'Love me, love my myth!' The art of loving seems to be the art of keeping a proper distance. To come right in and identify is to lose the help of another point of view. To keep right out is to lose the help of genuine sympathy and shared concern. But in experience it is impossible to maintain oneself for long at such a point of distance. It is the ideal golden mean which we pass through, in our happier moments, on our way in or our way out; as we seek to take the place of the object of love, giving ourselves over to feeling the same way from inside, and as we step back to size up from outside. One stance involves one kind of loss and gain, the other another kind. Such salvation and love as we can get comes by way of movement between the two, each time perhaps a little further in or a little further out, or in at a different angle and out at a different angle. Whether the object of love is a person, a myth or a field of study, such movement is its method; and the Christian is held to it by the archetypal symbolic pattern of Christ's movement which is the same. To put it in a static formula is bound to be as misleading as sticking to the ideal golden mean of distance. But, with that warning taken, it is arguable that the Christ-formulae of the church's councils, insisting with loud paradox on thorough divinity and thorough humanity, are as good a job as can be done in that line – always granted that that line is not mistaken for anything else and that the algebra of philosophizing on history is distinguished from the historical events it reflects upon, as well as attached to them.

A sense of maddening delicacy can overwhelm us as we prod into such orthodoxy: the sort of feeling induced by playing spillikins. So it is worth getting relief from taking note of what it is against as much as what it is for, and that can be put again in the single word 'obsession', which means getting hung up on one point and unable to move to another. The Christ-formulae cannot be possessed in static security, but they can serve as parameters of the movements which are all we can do. Similarly, myths serve to bring us nearer to God if we are interested in them without obsession. The mystics lead the way by grasping them and letting them go with their 'neither is this thou'. Like true poets, they are far from indifferent to the world of symbols. They get into it and explore it with thorough care. But they are always after something more than they have just grasped and said. They take God's immanence and intimacy so seriously as to address him in the familiarity of sensuous love lyrics. They take his transcendence so seriously as to cancel images and be silent before his strangeness. So Teilhard de Chardin on a more general plane:

> Why separate and contrast the two natural phases of a single effort? Your essential duty and desire is to be united with God. But in order to be united, you must first of all *be* – be yourself as completely as possible. And so you must develop yourself and take possession of the world *in order to be*. Once this has been accomplished, then is the time to think about renunciation, then is the time to accept diminishment for the sake of *being in another*. Such is the sole and twofold precent of Christian asceticism.[16]

It applies firmly to the use of myths. The God who is the object of this myth-using and myth-renouncing search is somehow congruent with it, as those testify who say that he is somehow *in* the searching. It is presented in the Christian myth-cum-antimyth of saving divine incarnation which is inexorably asserting its dominance over this discussion. The attractive splendour of divine being is expressed in the self-renunciation of it entailed by the interest in us which is love. To put it with mythological crudity and awkwardness, God is not obsessed by his own transcendent divinity. He loses it for the sake of other interests, 'for us men and for our salvation'. He goes for what is not 'him', the human world which the religious mind sees in sharp contrast to his *milieu*, so that, in response, we can be freed from obsession with our humanity and get interested in the divinity which is not exactly 'us'. Such a movement of reciprocal exchange, which is in at the heart of Christianity, apparently has to be put in some such mythical terms as these. But we must borrow the obstinacy of the mystics by asserting that it is also a sort of anti-myth, pointing away from itself and the august luxuries of the imaginative and ecclesiastical worlds to the duties and puzzles of everyday 'in which it pleaseth him to dwell'. So its true adherents are not so much those who abase themselves before it in obsessive fascination as those who follow its movement down and out. To break from the mythical to the practical language of salvation, these will be people who are as genuinely interested in other people and God being right and good as in themselves being so. Such people are no more plentiful on the religious scene than the industrial or political, and everywhere come under suspicion of disloyalty because other interests have deprived them of the force of one-eyed obsession with their sectional interest. Perhaps we may be saved from obsession by boredom – with the self-righteousness and rejoicing-in-evil (other people's) which first pervades its speeches and then destroys its capacity for intelligible speech, with its sectional ideologies and myths. Then, with that detachment achieved, could be the time for the self-denying myth which militates against divine, let alone human, privilege. The judgment, which in old time theology precedes salvation, nowadays often takes the form of the criticism of detachment, the analysis which precedes cure, in religion as much as anywhere else.

3

Symbols

❦

Symbols are the smaller units which make up the bigger unit of a myth: the people, places or props which are strung into the mythical story. With it they share in the grand business of hitching waggons to stars, facts to vision, and what is to what might be – and exploring connections between these pairs. They must have strong links with the world we already know in any case and with the world which we do not yet know and are exploring. Myths and symbols could both be put under the heading of 'fictions' if it were not so obviously misleading at first glance. At second glance any fiction, if it is at all intelligible, is seen to owe at least as much to the objective world of waggons as to the subjective one of stars. Novels can be realistic where sociological reports are symbolically abstract. Scientists explain that their occupation is not just a traffic in pure hard facts, as the man in the street supposes. Rather, it gets the energy and interest which advance it from the interplay of facts and imagination, so that the aesthetic term 'elegance' is high praise among them for a piece of work. By the same token, theology cannot be reduced to a trade in nothing but theories, because these are never beyond the reach and critical pressure of the brutal facts – medical, meteorological, economic, political, social – which shape them. It too lives and moves in an inextricable marriage of images and events, so that the theologian's life is something more strenuous and more fun than drifting among ideas and visions.

This state of affairs is nothing new to biblical scholars, church historians and philosophers of religion. The latest theological discipline, the sociology of religion, makes it more dramatically clear than ever. People in pews are helped by the news that doctrines and images have not dropped out of the sky but, like the rest of the furniture, have been made by particular peoples' efforts to realize their ideas, and have intelligible histories. The Christian theologian is particularly aware of it because the inherited tradition which is his material, and the faith by which he handles it, are both in a marriage of symbols and events where the differences are as vital as the union.

In this chapter symbols will be looked at mainly in the context of liturgies, or church services, in which they play a very large part, and where most Christian people have their biggest formative encounter with them. There are three other reasons.

1. Some restriction to a particular area is necessary to keep the discussion in some sort of shape, and a practical and accessible area like this is a reasonable choice. Here theology comes to life in a swarm of symbols.

2. After centuries of continuity in which one service book was the norm, more or less faithfully stuck to with unofficial variations, new services have been officially introduced into the major Western churches. In the Church of England there is choice, because the old services are still allowed and the new ones provide alternatives; in the Roman Catholic Church less so, because they have been banned. But even in this latter instance authority cannot ban peoples' memories of the old services. They still compare them in their minds. So a kind of relativity has been officially introduced into the sacred sphere of liturgy. We no longer consider it from one given standpoint but from several. Freedom to criticize and choose has got its foot into the church door, whether to be suppressed or allowed. And this critical choosing, assessment of the usefulness (old-style 'edification'), or practical value, of the symbols deployed in one form of service or another is the job which churchgoers share with pundits. The present discontinuity in liturgical traditions therefore provides a

monumental instance of the meeting of religion with criticism which this book is all about. Once we may have gone to church in child-like innocence to accept, wonder and dream:

> You are not here to verify,
> Instruct yourself, or inform curiosity
> Or carry report. You are here to kneel
> Where prayer has been valid.[1]

Now we have another basic duty, uncomfortably like that banned in Eliot's lines, to fit in with the acceptance and wonder. Churchgoing Adam has been presented by Eve, in her role as Mother Church, with the fruit which teaches discrimination.

3. The new services have not been so successful as to make either conservative people forget the old ones or modernizing people feel that the job of *aggiornamento* has really been done. It is hard to see how they could have been.

·It follows from these points that the crucial area of liturgy, where Christianity is most often encountered and the character of churches formed, is wide open. The governors of the churches are faced with the possibility of chaos, the indulgence of a vast range of whims – trendy, statesmanlike, or atavistic – and may find themselves reaching for such legal powers as they have to assist them in their duty of keeping order. But these are blunt instruments, wielded from outside the worshipping communities concerned and the reasons of the heart, so important in worship, which inform them. If they have to be used in an age when church life puts more emphasis on democratic than hierarchical authority it will, if at all possible, be later rather than sooner: after congregations and their hangers-on, whose more occasional church-going makes them even more impressionable about services, have had time to decide what they want. Yet if this is only to be done in terms of the reasons of the heart, the governors will have to wait a very long time for incomprehensibly vague answers. Gut reactions and whims, however fundamental, make bad bricks for community-building and decision-making if they are not allied to reasons of the head. However much of an intruder it may look in liturgy, the critical faculty is needed if the reasons of the heart are not to get lost in their own subjectivity or squashed by desperate authority. It is needed to examine, with critical appreciation, the symbols which make up services. Amongst other things, the examination will have to be historical, applying an informed sense of timing to the symbols; of how the world was when a symbol was born and flourished and how it is now. Two aspects of this are so daunting as to raise hopes that it can be put off. It looks irreverent ('tread softly, for you tread on my dreams'[2]) and it looks like a lot of hard work. So ways that promise to be easier are naturally tried first.

There is an indulgent conservative line which admits into a liturgy symbols which can prove their biblical origins. But it is not workable as a criterion of choice. In fact, and as always with the Bible, an unmanageably vast range which includes contradictions means that we pick and choose from it according to certain criteria, and it is these which call the tune. Even in christology they rule off, as we shall see later, much of the biblical Christ. Anybody can quote scripture; and church history makes very clear that to insist that people should do so is not to bring any kind of useful clarity or order into church life. What matters is why people choose the quotations they do, and that they themselves should acknowledge why.

Another easier way has a liberal character. If something in a liturgy is opaque and baffling, a question or a complaint about it is met by saying that it is symbolic or poetic. It seems to imply that with symbols anything goes, no questions asked, and order of any kind is less likely than ever. It is also on to something more serious. Symbols, it suggests, are august and mysterious entities, to be contemplated reverently rather than interrogated importunately. With them, as with royalty, we ought not to speak before we are spoken to. Confronted by the immense symbolism of St Peter's, Rome, or the St Matthew Passion, a person must at some point stop nagging and simply attend. But he would do well to precede that by reading works of critical investigation into them, even in the humble form of a guidebook or a programme note. And it would certainly be a sign that the symbols had meant something to him if he followed the encounter with the symbol with analytical inquiry about how it came to be so, for what social purpose it was originally used, how it relates to other works of the same maker and how to the aspirations of his patron or audience. These questions, too, will lead out of the child-like dreamworld in which things just *are* without question and into the grown-up world where symbols are made. Here people work, and the work consists of trying to manage the engagement of vision with practical possibility: how to keep one eye on the inward light and another on syntax, or the melting temperature of bronze, or a patron's impatience; how to get the limitlessness of *this* to terms with the constraints of *that* when they do not get on easily – but will both be better for being together. The workshop of symbols is not an airy place where men just dream of associations or dash things off in a fine frenzy, but a laboratory. A sign of the quantity of work and the excruciating standards entailed is the amount of waste lying about on the workshop floor. This is a world where the symbol which is nearly right will not do at all, where august pedigrees have to prove present value.

The most majestically assured symbols come out of this sort of hand-to-hand fighting. Their continued existence does not just depend on people revering them silently. They live because people continue to be on hand-to-hand terms with them; both hearing them and asking them questions in a conversation which helps both parties in the practical business of surviving so long as it is a real and necessary exchange.

Symbols have histories or biographies. None of them is eternal. Some of them have very long useful lives, which is not the same thing. Some are dead. Some are hibernating and not to be aroused before their time. And some, like Ahab in his chariot,[3] though terminal cases are propped up until the going down of the sun lest the army should lose heart and panic. Symbols in theology point to eternal things but are not eternal things themselves. They are historical and have times and seasons. So their pointing (which is their point) can be done at some times and not at others, goes through good days and bad days and alliances and break-ups like the rest of us; starts, develops and stops. To ignore this distinction between the life of a symbol and the life it indicates often looks honorific and pious but turns out, surprisingly, to be an act of disloyalty, a betrayal with a kiss. For example, Wordsworth's poetic diction in *Lyrical Ballads* and the human, divine and natural being which they indicate are separable. Somebody might be tempted not to think so because of the sheer and satisfactory wholeness of the poems, but that it is so will become clear if he succumbs practically to the temptation. He so reveres Wordsworth that he can think of nothing better than to use precisely his techniques to talk about nature and people in the twentieth century. The result is all too predictable; a literary dead duck or stuffed owl. It has come about because of what Cranmer in the liturgical context called 'bondage of the figure or shadow':[4] in other words, the simplistic belief that slavish imitation of Wordsworth might produce poetry as effective as his, and the refusal to take into account that 1978 is not the same time in poetry as 1798. For success the opposites are needed. Instead of literal imitation of a revered authority there has to be the disciplined freedom of the spirit in which poets have sons and not slaves. Instead of the ignoring of historical differences there has to be a good grasp of them, of how things were then and how they are now and how the two can or cannot relate. The same freedom and hard-headed sense of history is needed in the assessment of liturgical symbols. Liturgies are always second-hand and a remembrance of time past. Also, they are always for the present, astonishing their participants by shedding new light on their lives. The conjunction of these two things is extremely difficult to manage and all sorts of mistakes can result: mutton dressed up as lamb, or a liturgical equivalent of the reproduction furniture which belongs not to the past or the present but to a no-man's-land between the two. For so important an area something better is needed. It will be hard to find, but without a sound sense of history, of past and present, it will not be found at all.

The problems meet us head on in the most famous and familiar of symbolic phrases used in church services: 'Our Father which art in heaven'. At least, that is what everybody used to say. A little while ago the 'which' was reasonably changed to 'who'. Now the latest services offer us 'Our Father in heaven'. The whole thing goes right off the rails with the often-heard 'Heavenly Father'. In ordinary speech 'heavenly' is a word used for gushing praise: an apparently tiny snag which brings to a head the disjuction between church and ordinary world about 'heaven' which has been there for a long time. A titanic symbol seems to have met an iceberg which has been growing quietly for years, and it is time for an inquiry into the accident. An acute and deep dilemma emerges from it.

In its native past heaven was two things at once. It was both the sky, the solid if translucent roof where the stars were and the rain came from, and it was the realm of God. Simultaneously an agreed theological symbol and an agreed scientific 'fact', its symbolism worked because it engaged with how people saw their world in any case: and 'we do not live in a place but in a description of a place', whether as scientists or as religious believers, so it matters fundamentally that the description should be coherent and agreed – urgently so for a religion which claims universal and contemporary relevance. But now the 'agreed fact' partner-in-the-pact has changed out of all recognition. We just do not see the sky like that any more, and the modern translators of the Lord's Prayer acknowledge this tacitly by never translating the original Greek's *ouranos* as sky, though it would be formally allowable – and the faithful agree by being tacitly grateful that they do not. In the past there was a totality, a wholeness of interlocked describing-and-seeing of the world, for theological and scientific star-gazers: and it helped, for a long while, that astronomers were usually clergymen or astrologers. That totality, as such, has gone, but people who go to church to worship are unfailingly given remnants of it, with the result that their churchgoing and the rest of their making sense of the world are disjoined. In 1655 when a preacher, trying to get more breathing space for the problem, 'attempted to explain that Heaven was so high that a millstone would take hundreds of years to come down from it, one of his hearers asked how long in that case it would take a man to get up there'.[5] The testimony of this anecdote to the long standing of the problem does not help with it, because the same interval of time has been marked by decline in the hold of many of religion's old symbols over people's minds.

Christian readers will probably be bored and irritated by the rehearsal of all this, and justly protest that they have known about it for a long time. The trouble is that church services go on as if they did not, and the revision of them often makes things worse by scratching the problem and not either leaving it alone or curing it; so betraying not faith but unresolved, even unconscious, worry. Deeper down, the trouble is that people are being given shadows instead of solid religious food. The symptoms are of under-nourishment. In other words, it is a practical and pastoral matter.

The inquiry reveals the importance of the totality, of a wholeness of vision and description which, by all religious accounts, is so bound up with salvation and worship that without it they are scarcely possible. Symbols are ecological things. When their surroundings change, the more resilient and promising of them adapt and survive, the weaker vanish. Heaven seems to be an in-between case. It demonstrably survives because it is allied to the sense of God's transcendence which is deep in religious experience. Deprived of *rapport* with its secular partner, however, it clouds over and becomes opaque. It is enfeebled and does its job so badly that to the majority of people, with no ill-will and possibly with regret, it is baffling. Some people ('last survivors of the age of chivalry') have a sense that they cannot believe in God without it, more that they cannot believe in God with it. So anybody with a Christian conviction sincere enough for him to want to share it with others who may not be capable of following a course in cosmology is faced with a practical problem of what to do.

First, and on the practical small scale, tinkering revisions of the kind we noticed with the beginning of the Lord's Prayer may be worse than a waste of time. Without getting to the root of the trouble, they make it itch. They disturb the indispensable religious function of habit for insufficient reason.[6] Amongst other things, people certainly go to church to enter a world where, in contrast to the flux of ordinary life, 'all is accustomed, ceremonious'; to drink at ancient springs. Equally certainly they go because the rituals are illuminating, the springs refreshing. They are not so conservative as to refuse helpful changes. Until we have something new to say about God which is allied with new ways of seeing the world, there is something fundamentally wrong in talking about him, the subject and object of worship, in 'new' liturgies. As always when we lack what we want, a hopeful bearing of the lack is preferable in the long view to filling it up with *ersatz* substitutes.

The fading of 'heaven' is not, in any case, an unambiguous disaster. It does not serve the experience and doctrine of divine transcendence with complete success. Transcendent means 'beyond' rather than 'in some remote but accessible place'. Positing a location robs the doctrine of its essentially teasing quality which beckons and baffles (in a more profound and necessary sense) the religious mind. The loss of one makes us think of the doctrine in a more thorough-going and serious way which is more likely to induce the intended sense of awe than the vague concert hall, celestial city or park of traditional imagery. For something which by definition is beyond imagery, the loss of such symbols is even appropriate: God is more thoroughly transcendent than any religion and its symbolism can cope with. It has to testify to this by being wary of in-between entities and symbols. Christianity had plenty of testing practice in this as it argued out its central symbol of the doctrine of Christ. The temptation, strong because plausible, was to think of him as occupying some intermediate position between transcendent God and man. Such a figure was obviously meant to have a mediating religious function, but the sort of *tertium quid* which resulted – a being less awesome than God and more dignified than man and all too familiar in Christian imagination to this day – was too heavy a price in irrelevant nonsense to pay. It had to be asserted that he is both utterly divine and utterly human – what all symbols try to be but cannot. Long discussion of symbols had shown up their shortcomings and pushed discussion into an area beyond them. There was a price to pay, in coherence and imaginability, but a fatal mistake had been corrected. In religion it can be better to have majestic incoherence than trivialized coherence, to share Moses' 'O word, word that I lack' rather than Aaron's glib symbolic catering.[7]

A heightened and better sense of transcendence is one positive benefit which is available after the symbolic collapse of heaven. Another is a more thorough sense of divine immanence or pervasive presence in the world. God is more immanent than any religion can cope with. Heaven is not exactly a help here. By indicating God's *milieu* or home as a remote palace it implies that his relation to our world is like that of an eighteenth-century landlord, administratively preoccupied and based in London, who makes intermittent if momentous visits to his country heritage. This does not measure up to the experience of God as elusive because of his extreme, or ultimate, nearness, given to the Christian mystics who exclaim that 'my inmost I is thou', or to more ordinary people, such as Francis Kilvert the Herefordshire curate and diarist, sensing divinity in nature and human love with an immediacy which amazes them. Perhaps it would be better to change the image from landlord to peasant. Symbols which are working badly can be got going again by being stood on their heads. Is divine presence in the world more like that of the worker, bound to the land in an inexorable covenant, bettering and wounding to both parties and so close that, as was said of the countrywoman Beatrix Potter, it was not always possible when she stood still to distinguish her dumpy figure from the hillside boulders? It would certainly have liturgical point by positing a divinity who joins, by his presence, our world to himself. Which is what liturgy is about.

> All that matters is to be at one with the living God
> To be a creature in the house of the God of Life.

Lawrence's poem goes on to describe the mixture of homeliness and awe which constitutes worship.

> Sleeping on the hearth of the living world
> Yawning at home before the fire of life
> feeling the presence of the living God
> like a great reassurance
> a deep calm in the heart
> a presence
> as of a master sitting at the board
> in his own and greater being
> in the house of life.[8]

The symbol which does it is the hearth: an excellent one because it is an immemorially traditional centre of human life which is still there. Modern householders who lack it are induced to regret and rectify the lack by television advertisements for solid fuel (and even gas and electric) fires, presented with the same appeal of unifying and relaxing comfort, of gathering round the homely mystery of fire. To say the least, it works better than heaven as a contemporary-cum-traditional symbol of the ultimate home, the place of wonderful relaxation and (in the full sense) familiarity with a touch of awe. The emphasis is on this immanent aspect of divine presence. And this is a reason for the success of the image at a time (was there ever another?) when this aspect of divinity is understandably the most commonly grasped. Yet a sense of transcendence lifts the image from banality. It was set in the first two lines and returns in the last four, so containing the comfortable centre. The shortest line of the poem, 'a presence', brings it in with a brevity implying solemn silence. There is another, with us domestic animals, who is the master of the house of life 'in his own and greater being'. We are not alone and, if the house of life contains all, he is supreme in it as the centre which causes us to forget the previous central image of the fire. Once again an excellent image has been set up and then transcended.

Perhaps there are other reasons for forgetting Lawrence's image of the hearth – regretfully. We are talking about liturgy, and although it is an attractive possibility that it might conceivably find its place in a modern service book, that is less than likely. Christians have another symbol to which they are bound, both officially and in sincere emotional and intellectual obligation: the arch-symbol of Christ.[9] It fulfils a similar function. Round Christ human-kind is gathered, calmed and reassured, as the centre of the living household. Yet he, as image and presence, is willingly transcended into the presence of God as the centre to which he belongs, and to which we belong as gathered round him. When symbolism in Christian liturgy is the task, the immanent and transcendent presence of God must be explored in terms of him.

It has been a commonplace for some time among modern theologians to distinguish between the Jesus of history (then) and the Christ of faith (now). It is not a hard-and-fast or clean distinction, positing a complete discontinuity – something which would be made clearer if the talk were about 'the Jesus Christ' of history and of faith, instead of the usual dividing of name from title, apportioning one (Jesus) to history and one (Christ) to contemporary faith. The value of the distinction is to point out that two ways of talking about Jesus Christ are open to us in Christian theology. He can be spoken of as belonging to the past, which gives a necessary objective-feeling reference; and as belonging to the present, which gives a necessary subjective-feeling reference. It is more complicated than that, as the next chapter on the presence of Christ will explore, but in this rough form it is valid and useful. For the trouble with so many services and service books is that reference to Jesus Christ, which is obligatory and sustaining to Christians, turns time and again, and all but automatically, into reference to the past so relentless as to begin to look obsessional: which is not quite so obligatory or sustaining. Reference to the past is not being denied. It will still, unassailably, be there. But we can leave it alone for a little longer and be the better for it. For example, it is said in

the thanksgiving prayer of the Anglican Series 3 Communion Service that 'through Jesus Christ' God 'created
all things', 'freed us from the slavery of sin', 'made us a
people for his own possession'. Past tenses throughout
give a sense of objectivity at the price of distance. If these
proclamatory assertions are changed into the present tense,
the gain in immediacy is clear. Through Jesus Christ God
creates all things, frees us, makes us a people. Nor is this
just arguably better liturgical theatre. It is arguably better
doctrine too. Creation, redemption and new community:
these are not things over and done in Christian doctrine,
but divine-human (hence 'through Jesus Christ' as the
symbolic principle of that) work in progress: and some of
that work is done in worship. In the doctrine of John's
gospel these are events equidistant from all points of time,
as is the Christ who is so present to every man, whether
Abraham or the contemporary Christian, that the apostolic
generation had no religious advantage.

All that is suggested here is a redressing of the balance
to suit worship as an activity which is always a remembrance
of things past *and* for the present, a correction of a lop-
sidedness betrayed by a slight note of obsession. And it
is within Christian tradition that something can be done
to rectify it: which, for a churchman, is cheering. The
makers of the new service were, like all Christians, selective
in their use of the riches of tradition. Once the tendency
of the selection has been spotted it can be corrected by
a conscious leaning the other way, like oarsmen balancing
a boat. The same thing needs to be done with another
aspect of the liturgical presentation of Christ: an aspect
which is highlighted by asking the question 'Who is Christ
for?'

Again, traditional Christian theology gives two answers.
He is for everybody. He is for the church. Both are found
in the New Testament, with the emphasis now on one
and now on the other. In Paul's letters he mystically lives
in Christian individuals and community, but in the
fulfilment of the final End – which for Paul was pressingly
imminent – includes all humanity. In the first three gospels
most space is given to Jesus' energetically eclectic career

of teaching and healing, including power over the world's
governing natural and supernatural forces and going
beyond Jewish boundaries.[10] He is portrayed in the
landscape of the world at large. Less space, and in Mark
practically none, is given to the founding and forming of
the Christian church. In John the weight is reversed. The
world and 'the Jews' are an outer darkness, for all that
'God so loved the world', around the illuminated fold of
believers to which everybody belongs in principle, though
the absence of an eschatology as strong as Paul's makes
this hazy. John's tendency is betrayed in the text, since
made familiar by war memorials, 'greater love hath no
man than this, that he lay down his life for his friends'.
On the contrary, there is a greater love than this sublime
esprit de corps, and the first three gospels present it: that
of the man who lays down his life for his enemies. At
least one soldier on each side in the First World War knew
it: Eric Maria Remarque who wrote *All Quiet on the Western
Front*, and Wilfred Owen, the Christian outside the church
who wrote 'Strange Meeting' and 'At a Calvary on the
Ancre'.[11] Neither of them would have been impressed by
the Johannine war memorial's seeming support for 'us'
against 'them'.

Granted that both views are Christian, which do we
choose for leader? The choice cannot be dodged, even by
making it surreptitiously, and more often than not the
churches have gone for the Johannine option. It is obviously
more definitively organizing, and has the promise of
spiritual privilege unspoiled by the mess of life unillumi-
nated and unredeemed. The usual pattern of priority has
Christ as centre surrounded by the church, beyond which
is the world. It governs the Series 3 Communion Service.
We, the baptized church-people, are the body of Christ,
the people of God's own possession, and pray accordingly:
first for the church as 'we', then for people in politics or
ill as 'men' or 'them'. We pray for our friends but not
our enemies, though Jesus told us to (Matthew 5.44). In
the context of such incipiently possessive spirituality it is
not surprising to find the symbol of Christ as 'our great
high priest' presented in defiance of the historical fact

that the totality it belongs to (Jewish temple worship) was destroyed in AD 70, so it is in a worse symbolic plight than 'heaven', and that its applicability to so unclerical a figure as the Jesus of the first gospels is ambiguous. But then little or nothing is heard here of the Jesus of the first three gospels: not even their obviously appropriate theme of his sitting at table with religion's outsiders. The symbolism of the Christ of church and creeds far outweighs the symbolism of the Christ for others.

It is difficult for two reasons not to think that a wrong choice, of doctrinal priorities and concomitant symbols, for the present time has been made.

The first reason is founded in critical analysis. The church may like to think of itself as so different from other institutions as to be in some sense outside 'the world', but historians and sociologists refuse to co-operate. It is precisely as a human institution that it attracts their attention, appreciative and critical. The work of Christopher Hill and his pupil Keith Thomas[12] on seventeenth-century English Christianity thrives by refusing to lay down historical-sociological tools. Christians may argue with their methods and views but not, while they appeal to the historical character of their religion, declare them invalid on principle, even when they capitalize on Marxism. If Christian symbolism and doctrine is to fulfil its universal saving function in the present day, it has to be by engagement with, rather than disengagement from, such disciplines. It has, in other words, to love its 'enemies' in the sense of being intellectually and emotionally interested in them, which entails letting them influence its way of living and seeing itself. 'To see ourselves as others see us' is a divine gift entailed in *the* divine gift of charity. The alternative is the fundamentally implausible spectacle of a declining enclave making immense claims for itself, fearful of the world beyond and seeing in Christ, its central symbol, the reflection of its own institutional face.

The second reason for dissatisfaction with over-ecclesiastical christology is continuous with the first, but comes more from ordinary observation and common sense than academic inquiry. People live in a world where there are religious believers of many institutional allegiances and more of none. Sociological surveys endorse their observation. Such a setting does not rule out of court any religion's claims to have saving truth about God for mankind. 'Lord, we are few but thou art near', the Christians sing and are not contradicted. But are they uniquely and decisively nearer than everyone else, than Gandhi and Dubcek, Martin Buber and the saints of Sufism? There, contradiction is more likely and defensible. If it is allowed at all, what happens to the central and integrating Christian symbol of Jesus Christ as the human-divine actuality?

The question is urgent and majestic. To begin an answer it seems best to take a few steps back behind the ecclesiastical symbolism of Christ (and Christ as ecclesiastical symbol) by asking how Jesus became a universal and saving symbol in the first place; in other words, how the Jesus Christ of particular history and of general faith are connected.

1. According to the undeniable witness of the gospels Jesus was a Jew, but not an ordinary rank-and-file or institutionally biddable one. Jewish tradition was nourishingly, and confiningly, available to him. His head and heart were apparently as permeated by the precepts and symbols of the ancient scriptures as any Pharisee's. But while he took the nourishment he refused the confinement. An acute and immediate sense of the presence of people and God carried him through its boundaries and beyond, to explore the universal things of common humanity, to respond to them and the immediately present ('abba') Father afresh and more deeply. Nor was this exactly 'once for all' in the sense that it would not need anyone to do it again. He laid the same way on his followers with the commandment to love God and neighbour, which relativized religious practice and allegiance as subsidiary. Like him they were obliged, in the present face of God as One and All, to reach those parts which religion, in its intermediate position, was not affecting. It put him, and he promised that it would put them, on uneasy terms with traditional religion. Being part of it (and so, loyal) and being concerned

with other imperative interests (and so disloyal), he and they were the kind of people whom the governors find more irritating than the rank outsiders.

2. While this general scope, making the world his parish, is essential for a man to be a helpful universal symbol, it is not enough in itself. The general good becomes the excuse of the bully, the liar and the hypocrite if it keeps clear of 'minute particulars'. Theoretical talk about the general good gets nobody into trouble, as preachers have often observed in this context. It has to be worked out in patient engagement with everyday detail, and then trouble is assured. It is, again, the undeniable witness of the gospels that Jesus got deep into the detail and the trouble, and that this, which was the end of him as a man, was the indispensable beginning of him as a, or the, symbol.

This combination of serenely generous scope with particular, agonized engagement makes the universal and healing human symbol. The high doctrines, although they necessarily follow and we find them in Paul's earliest reflections on Christ, are secondary explorations of it from the historical point of view, though philosophically they can claim to describe its basis. They have, like all such developments, a tendency to isolate and exclude as they help to form the institution necessary to having a distinct place in the world. So there is a long-standing tendency for Christians to work against Jesus' outgoing scope by asserting that nobody else has achieved the combination described, and he is put on an isolated institutional pedestal. But if this were completely appropriate, Jesus, as man become (or *cum*) divine symbol, would not be as intelligible as he is. We understand him, and are daunted by the demanding relevance of what we understand, because we know of others like him – and are potentially not so unlike him ourselves, according to him. His double commandment to love God and neighbour, summing up and overriding religion, is precedented in the Old Testament and paralleled in the rabbis who shared his concern for practical simplicity. The Stoics of his day had a religion of inclusive universal scope based on monotheism and human brotherhood. Martin Luther King, Bonhoeffer, the fictional Dorothea of George Eliot's *Middle-march*, Rabbi Johannan ben Zakkai, Gandhi and thousands more have worked out their ideals in the minute particulars of the politics of nations or the country town. The kind of singular and compound uniqueness which is often applied to Christ, and means something different from the uniqueness of the exceptional individual, comes perilously near to unintelligible irrelevance, however necessary it has been to the church's self-establishment. How could we understand a completely one-off being as a human being and, as such, relevant to us? The point has been made to me pastorally. Trying to comfort a troubled person by telling her that Jesus had a terrible time too, I got a sharp rejoinder. Jesus was God's only Son. He could have summoned legions of angels to get him out of trouble: and even if he did not, knowledge of the possibility was a boost for morale not available to her. He had things 'which in your case you do not have'.[13] High doctrines have their price and pay it.

They have not, however, been brushed aside: except temporarily while we look at the historical reason for them. Having done that we can be better placed to find saving help in them. The idea of the uniqueness of Christ is not just an institutional safeguard and source of superior comfort. Holding on to the sources of Jesus' symbolic power, the immediacy of depth and scope, the engagement with detail, we can see that there is a sort of uniqueness here which chimes with the central Christ myth of the descent of divine being and does not supersede it. There has never been a shortage of people persuaded that they are unique, from conquering kings to lowly people in their testy or euphoric moments, or to anybody incredulous of the certainty of his own death. This is all too banal and symbolically the reverse of helpful, let alone saving. Another sort of person helps and saves because he attains uniqueness by forgetting it for other interests. There is a legend of the Holy Grail, a symbol of Christ, which many knights set out to find. The one who attained it was he who, having come to its shrine and having it within reach, turned to its guardian, noticed the unhealed and putrefying wound which afflicted him and asked how it was with ·him. He who loses glorious uniqueness for the sake of its apparent opposite of commonplace misery, gains it. And only he because only he is fitted for it. The legend is an apt parallel to the Christ myth. It is all too intelligible and directs attention to an essential characteristic of the helpfully unique person: his dedication to the commonplace. For many musicians and listeners Mozart occupies a unique place, not just for his extraordinary talents but because he used them to plumb the depths of the sadness and happiness which everybody knows. Tamino in *The Magic Flute* comes to salvation through trial because he is a man and, lest we should be misled by Tamino's noble character, Papageno gets there too and for the same reason – although he is not noble at all and (which is very important) does not for a moment pretend that he is. As in Jesus' teaching, saints and sinners belong together, to the exclusion of the outraged self-righteousness of the Queen of the Night who, according to some commentators, represents institutional religion. And we find ourselves back at the self-denying centre as the source of salvation: with uniqueness, in a surprisingly self-deprecating attitude, witnessing to it.

The final question is practical. How can this symbol of the self-denying centre, the central Christian symbol uniting divinity and humanity which is presented in the doctrinal myth of incarnation, be worked out in worship? Bonhoeffer's question, 'who Christ really is for us today?' needs to be worked out in liturgical terms with more attention to his conviction that Christ is the centre of life: not just for ' "last survivors of the age of chivalry", or a few intellectually dishonest people on whom we can descend as "religious" ', but for everybody. According to him it is a job for church people 'not regarding ourselves . . . as specially favoured, but rather as belonging to the whole world'. This is precisely the need which has been shown up by our critique of liturgy. It points us away from ecclesiastical self-concern and the christology which goes with it, towards the discovery of Christ in the world. The

ominous thing about this for church people is that it is
a movement away from the area in which they are at
home and in some sort of control, and towards some sort
of untidy pantheism: an unwelcome word in church circles
after the long hiatus in natural theology which followed
two world wars. But there is a more urgent and more
strictly theological question which has to be asked before
attending to such fears. Will such a movement help or
hinder the love of God and neighbour; take us nearer to
the God of Jesus Christ or further from him?

The Jesus of the first three gospels was, by the strictest
orthodox standards, something of a pantheist, and appeals
to people because of it. He saw the immediacy of God in
the immediacies of the world. The tensions and fulfilments
of family life, trade, agriculture and politics were the stuff
of his message; the possibility of divine salvation in any
human life its aim. This 'closeness to nature' was a beloved
theme of yesterday's liberal teachers and preachers. It may
be *passé* in academic fashion and play a negligible part in
creeds and the texts of church services, but it says
something fair about the Christ of Matthew and Luke –
and something which appeals intelligibly to people
mystified by the arguments of academics and ecclesiastics.
On these grounds it is entitled to more than standing
room in the church, the odd hymn or sermon. 'We bless
thee for our creation, preservation, and all the blessings
of this life.' 'We praise thee, O God, for thy glory
displayed in all the creatures of the earth. . . . All things
affirm thee in living.'[14] It is not a minor catastrophe that
such praise of common-or-garden glory is sold short in
some of the modern services, and it is not at all difficult
to supply the lack.

It may be objected that in Christian tradition the presence
of God is not seen in the birds and the bees but in man.
However grudging this is in comparison with some of the
gospel teaching of Jesus, it has force from the point of
view of the church's teaching which followed his. 'The
glory of God is a living man.' Yet here too the expansiveness
of glory forces a wider view such as that taken by Geoffrey
Lampe:

Salvation is not a future act of God which has still to begin;
it has been, and is, in progress from the beginning of the
creation of man. God has always been incarnate in his human
creatures, forming their spirits from within and revealing
himself in and through them; for although revelation comes
from beyond the narrow confines of the human spirit and is
not originated by man himself, there is not, and never has
been, any revelation of God that has not been incarnated in,
and mediated through, the thoughts and emotions of men
and women.[15]

This, in turn, may be suspected of the optimistic geniality
which softens liberalism, but the suspicion would be
unjust. The men and women of whom Lampe speaks have
become incarnate showings of God through suffering
pushed to the point of tragedy (Moses, Job, Jeremiah,
Paul, to keep to the Bible), which is their entitlement to
participation with Christ. The sort of Pan-Christism which
is being argued for here does not by-pass the cross but
puts it in the middle.[16] G. M. Hopkins used it to explore
the natural as well as the human world in terms of divine
presence. His poem 'The Windhover' begins with awe-
struck bird watching, 'the mastery, the achieve of the
thing!', but turns on the falcon's stooping descent as 'a
billion times told lovelier', a greater revelation of glory like
the 'blue bleak embers' in the fire-grate which 'fall, gall
themselves, and gash gold-vermilion'.

The symbols in Christian tradition are so numerous, to
put it mildly, that choice simply has to be exercised in
getting to grips with them. The kind of choosing that has
gone on in this chapter has attempted to be governed by
a sense of history and of the practical religious needs of
worship. Religious people do not like choosing any more
than other people. It is this which makes a book token
an agonizing if welcome present: one is haunted by the
fine things one has not picked. But the innate conservatism
of religion ensures that they will still be available for a
long time to come. If such symbols as heaven and the
great high priest have to be left behind in the totalities
they belonged to, because ours is not a place where they
can function properly, it should not be a matter for more
than a twinge of remorse. For the central Christian symbol

of Christ as the divine-human focus, to which they have done service in their times, survives energetically. Its drama of a divine movement downwards and outwards, a myth self-driven into the incarnation of historical action, the conceptualizing of it in a remorseless insistence on full humanity and full divinity, these are bound to, even meant to, give a sense of vertigo and agoraphobia to us as institutionalized believers, but to us as believers set in our world and time it brings company and salvation as well: the company of Lawrence, two Eliots, Hopkins and innumerable equally and less articulate people; the salvation of being reunited in lively interest to God and our neighbours.

One last note may serve to exemplify the practicality of the approach. It is often difficult for the churches' spokesmen, not least in the winter of 1979 when this is written, to know what to say to a disordered society: and they sense a duty to say something. Sectional interests dominate and are relentlessly pursued to the damage of everybody else. This is wrong and causes a revulsion which makes condemnation of it acceptable – but how effective? Yet again some critical investigation behind the scene is helpful. Photographs and television films showed pickets 'holding the country to ransom' in a curiously jovial frame of mind. In bitterly cold weather they stamped cheerfully around their bonfires in the intervals between lorries. Discordantly, they were enjoying something. What, is not far to seek. In a confused and chilly world they had discovered the *camaraderie* of struggle for their corporate good: something not a hundred miles from the comfort which people in the spiritually similar world of late antiquity found in religion, and which some people today find there too. 'The more we are together, the merrier we shall be', and the world is well lost in the cause. It is the we/them spirit of which we have found unmistakable traces in the more respectable context of church services as an expression of Christian togetherness. It is something which religious people know about. They have done their varieties of the picketing which makes controlling barriers. Excommunication has been their blacking. So when they fulfil their duty of saying something about it all, churchmen are first clear that they are not speaking *de haut en bas* but as sinners to sinners. Their institution is no stranger to restrictive practices which sort ill with divine love and human brotherhood. The power of the trade unions' special relationship with the Labour Party is put in the shade by the self-preserving force which the church got from its special relationship with the Roman emperor and his monarchical successors. As a result it is difficult, on this wicket, to see the church's relation to the world as being at all special in the sense of privilege allowing criticism of the specks in other people's eyes. It has, historically, a beam in its own. By an irony which it is tempting to think providential, the complaints of the Anglican clergy about the industrial scene were quickly followed by the Church Commissioners awarding them large, if much needed, rises in pay. So the relationship is more like that of two drunks companionably seeing one another home than of a morally superior ticking off a morally inferior person. If the church has an advantage, it is that it finds that the effects of deep draughts of 'sectional interest' are beginning to wear off it – not by its own wish or design – while leaving it enough of a headache as a withdrawal symptom to remind it of its participation in the disreputable party. Christian people have begun to learn that the championing of their sectional interests over against other people's is uncreative. Churches are learning to be practically and intellectually ecumenical, and dipping their toes in a 'wider ecumenism' which includes religions other than Christian and aspirations not specifically religious at all. They are finding it more interesting than *esprit de corps* and more wholesomely enjoyable. It has more of faith in divine and human possibility, and less of law, than the accustomed and natural way. A leading factor of it has been the self-relativizing which comes from a sense of the incompleteness of their sectional interest and the value of other people's – the sense of 'one world'. It is at this point that grace breaks in and begins to make inroads on the restrictive rigidities of law and moral recrimination, grace being the theologian's term for the divine gift of understanding participation without restriction. It is not something which a churchman can wheel in, but he can invoke it by putting himself and his neighbour in the right position, which is penitence in the communion of sins. In terms of Christ it parallels the moment at which he stepped down into the waters of John Baptist's baptism of corporate repentance: in gospel story the moment of the beginning of the new community. This chapter has been a long-winded attempt to bring Christian symbolism to the same moment.

4
Time and the Presence of Christ

The subject is still the same. We have two ways of looking at our world. If Wallace Stevens was right, we do not live so much in a place as in a description of a place, which is near to saying that we have two worlds. One is a realm of subjective dream, theory and myth, the other a realm of objective analysis, experiment and historical time. It is as if there were two worlds. Yet we know the world is one, and so these two occupy the same place. Christianity insists on the union as central. The two worlds interact constantly like a long-married couple. So long as Jack Sprat eats no imaginative fat and his wife eats no factual lean the platter is clean and peace reigns – at the expense of there not being any symbols or very much exciting communication. But in Judaism and Christianity, and perhaps most poignantly in Christianity, this relaxed idyll is not the norm. Here we have timeless myth claimed as having happened at particular points in time, historical study which expects to issue in some vision of abiding and timeless truth. So the two intersect, and the common territory, if it is the area of salvation, is also the scene of painful arguments. It is not only those who profess and call themselves Christians who are tangled up in this. Marxists are, too, as are most historians, critics and creators. Perhaps we all are. It is not, in any case, an occasion for regret or self-pity, because this interaction is at the centre of Christianity and stops either party going completely idiotic in the precise sense of the word. The interaction also stimulates imaginative adventure and art, as can be seen from the writings of the New Testament, which amount to a surprisingly diverse and vigorous theological renaissance, energized by the relation of these two worlds. It is a relation which promotes problems as well as creativity, which makes the problems which are necessary to get the creative adrenalin running.

Perhaps the most acute and divisive of these problems concerns the nature of Christ, presented as historical and timeless, mortal and abiding. Both these vital aspects of Christianity's view of its central figure were used in the last chapter in an attempt to understand him as an individual point of historical engagement who became a universal, saving symbol. It was done under the opposite pressures of criticism and institutional tradition. If some-. thing of religious value was established in the process, it is now time to put the pressures on again. The sense of history which was necessary to a just and liberating appreciation of myths and symbols must be put in the ring with the common, and even integral, conviction among Christians that when they meet to worship he is there among them, 'the contemporary Christ'.[1]

This is more surprising and incongruous than Christians usually seem to realize in a religion which prides itself on being emphatically historical, trains its adherents to think historically and has promoted so much good history writing. For the most basic, banal and serious thing about history is that it is about the passage of time in which men, ideas and even hardware come and go, all irrevocably. 'Time', they sing, 'like an ever-rolling stream, bears all its sons away.' Perhaps, as often, they don't give critically serious assent to what they are singing, or, if they do, silently make one saving exception among those sons. The hymn-line takes history seriously, and if seriously applied to the central focus of Christianity, Christ, could cause discomfort and edginess. Which, in turn, could lead into new creativity.

So here are two awkward bedfellows: in the same religion and fastened to the same central figure of Jesus

Christ, a claim to eternal truth which is the same yesterday today and for ever, and a claim to historical truth which cannot escape from change, in which things live by changing. 'Christianity is always adapting itself into something that can be believed' (T. S. Eliot). Which means that it survives as a going concern by adjusting to progress in science, historical and literary analysis, at least so much as not to be incredible from the standpoint of the mythology and the critical disciplines of the day. At the same time, it is reasonable to expect that it should still recognizably be Christianity. Which means that there must be some continuity running through all the switches and contradictions like an unbroken thread. And this is a function of the doctrine of the presence of Christ, to assert that the religion which Christians have after nineteen centuries of adaptation and development still has the same centre. But what kind of sense does it make?

The question cannot be addressed from a neutral standpoint because the issues are both too deep and too universal for anyone who cares enough to argue about them to be neutral.

The difficulty was felt already by the later New Testament writers. In those days before the establishment of Christian orthodoxy a man took his own line and its consequences, and it is important to this discussion to see how divergent are the lines taken by the two later gospel writers, Luke and John. Luke was very much the historian: not so much from the modern point of view of impeccable accuracy (he gets dates wrong) as in the more fundamental sense of taking time seriously. As Conzelmann discovered, he saw Jesus at the middle of time in a linear sense.[2] Before Jesus were the centuries of the Old Testament when he was prophesied but not present; after him the era of the church, which Luke wrote up in the first church history of the Acts of the Apostles. There Jesus is contemporary, but not exactly present because he is up in heaven: not living incarnately in his body the church or in the hearts of faithful individuals as for Paul, but up where Moses and Elijah have gone before him but where Luke's readers are not yet. Very occasionally he is seen there, as by the dying Stephen, or heard from there, as by the dismounted Paul. But ordinarily and usually the church gets on resoundingly well without him in the mystical-indwelling sense. It tells his story and finds its patterns repeated in its own; it has the energy of the spirit and knows itself to be guided in surprising detail by divine providence. Luke, as a writer with his nose to the grindstone of history, does not use a doctrine of Christ mystically or mysteriously abiding in the church or in the hearts of the faithful. John is quite different. His over-riding loyalty is to the realm of abiding truth, where some Jews philosophically interested in wisdom had found common ground with Gentiles indebted to Plato. If Jesus is in heaven, united to his Father, then so are his faithful people, reborn out of the world of flesh and blood into eternal communion with him and the Father. His Jesus was and is always present. 'Before Abraham was, I am', he says, and, 'Abraham rejoiced to see my day'. So those previous centuries are collapsed into the eternal now of the incarnate word. On the other side of the Christ-event, he says to Thomas after his resurrection, 'Blessed are those who (unlike Thomas and his contemporaries) have not seen and yet believe'. It is, that means, of no consequence religiously to have been about in Palestine between AD 1 and 30. History is not bunk, but it is reduced to eternal archetypal instances. It is symbolic – quite clearly in those hymns of abstract myth about light and darkness, truth and lies, father and son; but just as much in the psychological realism of his historical incidents. He achieves a depth of human penetration hitherto unprecedented in the gospels when he presents Nicodemus, the Samaritan *femme fatale* at the well, Caiaphas, Pilate and Thomas himself. These are deftly drawn faces of characters who are always with us, of perennial religious types. Here are the muddled sentimentalist and the sceptical realist, the ecclesiastical statesman whose duty is care for the machine rather than for truth, the politician whose principled neutrality goes down the plug hole of accelerating intrigue. John has a strong doctrine of the eternal presence of Christ, and he gets it by treating history not in Luke's

linear way but as a circle. All points of it, whether
Abraham of old or his readers today, are equidistant from
Christ who is the light for every man – for anyone who
can come out of the world's dark undergrowth and bear
to stand by the inextinguishable fire in the clearing. We
should perhaps say rather that there are two circles: an
inner one of light, an outer of darkness. By Luke's
standards, which are much more like ours as historians,
this is not really history at all, but history subjected to
philosophical theology. We can see the difference in their
parables: for Luke the realistically time-structured stories
of the Prodigal Son and Good Samaritan, for John the
timeless allegories of the vine and the sheepfold which
speak of eternal coinherence and exclusion.

The contrast of these two early Christian masters does
not solve the problem of a religion which claims to be
both historically and timelessly true, but it sets it with
remarkable clarity. We may be able to resolve it; on the
other hand, we may have – though as religious people we
still hate this as much as anybody – to choose.

Let me put the dilemma as clearly as possible by
following their examples and propounding a parable,
drawn out of the Sunday morning experience of a
churchgoer.

To get to church he passes through the churchyard.
There time rules. The tombstones bear names that mean
nothing whatever now, though once they were 'dearly
beloved'; and from many the names have been erased by
centuries of rain. They are decorated, too, with the badges
of the triumph of time and death: the hour-glass, the skull
and bones, the old man with his wings and scythe. There
are thinkers, seers and poets hanging about here, contem-
plating truths which we cannot and shall not escape:
Thomas Gray meditating on transience and Thomas Hardy
watching rain pour from a gargoyle on to the grave of
Fanny Robin.

Then he gets into church. Perhaps the only unambiguous
witnesses to time here are the dates on the memorial
tablets; the old man has, quite literally, been pushed to
the wall, and the churchgoer will only look at these traces

of his inexorable activity if his attention wanders from the central business of the service. And that is an eternal and present communion, 'triumphing over death and chance, and thee, O time'.[3] Hymns celebrate and instil a sense of the once-historical but now intimately accessible Jesus, guiding, accompanying and comforting. The scriptures are read for their present usefulness and effect and not, as in the historical critic's study, for interesting information about the past. They may well be read in a modern translation which is meant to bring them up to date. Incidentally, can we detect in recent face-lifting translations the old determination to contradict the passage of time in which things, as a matter of fact, get older and older and pass away? Anyhow, the service over, the churchgoer must make his way through the churchyard again to the world he ordinarily inhabits, and what is he to make of the outing? What does the relentless passage of time do to belief in the presence of Christ? How can this belief cope with the passage of time?

The question is put with that bias, giving the initiative to the 'time' rather than the 'eternity' party, for two reasons. The first is that a choice is needed, for the time being anyhow, if the argument is to maintain any sort of clarity. So Luke's way is chosen rather than John's, the linear everyday rather than the circular sublime, the timed rather than the timeless. The second is that for a religion which is meant for everyday and everybody rather than a sublime few, the asking of basic human questions before giving lofty answers is a strong entitlement. Man is timed and most of his business is trivial. He moves with the clock and through the diary. He confronts with eyes as clear as they can be the certain fact of death. He has to be faithful in little things if he is to be faithful in great. Or, using John's own more resonant version of the same idea, if he is told earthly things and will not believe, how will he believe heavenly things? And the church ought to be with him: not sweeping basic questions like this under the righly patterned carpet of institutional dogma, but sharing (indeed, realizing that it has no alternative to sharing) in the day of small things. That is where faith

is tested, for nearly all of us nearly all the time. Implicit
here is a promise. There is hope of coming by this route
to two grand topics of traditional Christian theology: a
genuine, as opposed to a denominationally qualified,
catholicism; and the discovery of something about the
working in history of the Spirit. But they are for later.

What is a Christian to do that will keep faith with both
the historical character of his belief, bound up with that
which is long ago and different, *and* its present power for
him, bound up with that which is the same and for ever.
Particularly, how is he to connect Jesus the first-century
Jew with Jesus the living focus of the twentieth-century
cult?

An attractively sensible solution has been put forward
by C. F. D. Moule.[4] Jesus, he says, 'spoke out of a
thought world very different from ours'. There he is with
the poet Louis MacNeice who, before teaching classics,
reflected glumly that,

> How one can imagine oneself among them,
>   I do not know
> It was all so unimaginably different
> And all so long ago.[5]

And he is taking up the point made with insistent clarity
by D. E. Nineham in *The Use and Abuse of the Bible*.[6] In
particular, says Moule, Jesus expected the end of the world
very soon and believed in demonic possession. We have
no common ground with him there, except at the price
of joining the Christian lunatic fringe – as Moule courteously
forebore to point out. Time has done its work here so
thoroughly that we cannot as twentieth-century people
with life insurance policies (which are decidedly practical
denials that next month will probably be exploded into
God) and medicines for epilepsy (which similarly deny
demon-possession) follow such antique drums. Yet many
other things about Jesus, his sayings, deeds and destiny,
still find and search us: so that we want to say with Eliot
that

> the communication
> Of the dead is tongued with fire beyond the language of the
> living.[7]

How? Such a thing must be based on a continuity in being human which exists along with the mutability. Moule refers to 'continuities which make the hermeneutical task possible', which means that there is enough in common between us and the dead for their relics and records to be useful to us if we interpret them ('the hermeneutical task') aptly. The virtue of this argument, in terms of the rules devised for the game, is that it can be set to work outside Christian doctrine as well as inside. Reading Byron's letters or Jane Austen's novels, one's pleasure at being on holiday in a world other than our own in every respect is joined by the pleasure of being in company with men of like passions and problems with ourselves and our neighbours for all the differences. Listening to Mozart's music can bring a strong sense of his personal presence, and if this looks like errant spiritualism we can appeal to no less orthodox a theologian than Karl Barth. He had an experience of that presence which was real enough during the Mozart bicentenary celebrations of 1956, and recorded it in a characteristically teasing vein. 'In one concert in the Basle Musiksaal, at which Clara Haskil was playing the F major concerto, I even had a sudden vision of him standing there in front of the piano, so clear that I almost began to cry. That's quite a story, isn't it – such a story that even Balthasar with his mystical experiences listened respectfully when I told him. At any rate, now I know just what Mozart looked like in the last year of his life!'[8] Brigid Brophy, whose standpoint is far removed from Barth's, has noticed the expression on the faces of listeners during the intervals of performances which seem to say '*my* Mozart', and so testify to some sort of personal communion.

So it is common experience, nourished by many and diverse instances, that there can be communion with the past. But how can one know just what or who has come through? Being a modern man can result in a reading of the Bible, Beowulf or Byron that would be unintelligible to, or at least was not intended by, the writers. Yet to be paralysed by this into supposing that only those original intentions are valid is to fall into the 'intentionalist fallacy', which stakes all on the undiscoverable and balks creativity. It even contradicts the intention that any serious writer has, to give members of the public a pattern of symbolic actions for them to make their own by exploring it. And it tries to skirt the one certain thing about such writing, that once it has been published it is public property. T. S. Eliot was asked at a party what he meant by his line 'Lady, three white leopards sat under a juniper tree'.[9] He replied, after a judicious pause, 'I meant "Lady, three white leopards sat under a juniper tree" ' – simultaneously defending his right to say what he said and leave it, and his interlocutor's duty to make of it what he could. The anecdote is a version of Pilate's 'what I have written, I have written',[10] with its ironically implied ' – and what you make of it is your business'. Glyndebourne's 1977 production of Mozart's *Don Giovanni* is an informative instance of the relations of text and interpretation because the process of its coming-to-be has been recorded in a book.[11] There was Mozart's score of da Ponte's libretto, but it poses a notorious problem of comedy or tragedy – amongst other problems. There were the reflections on its meaning of Hoffmann and Kierkegaard, but if they helped they did not solve. So when cast, designer, producer and conductor met, the whole thing had to be tackled afresh in the complicated, time-bound interaction which makes up the story of the book of the progress of the production of the opera: which is not accidentally like the rhyme 'This is the House that Jack built'. One thing that carried through the whole process of the production was, interestingly enough, the producer's conviction that the force of the opera would best be served by setting it in a period some twenty years later than its composition. A lot more was deliberately left to be worked out between producer and musicians in rehearsal. And the validity of it – that was something for audiences and critics to decide when the makers had finished. And what had they seen and heard? Mozart's *Don Giovanni*. But interpreted by a producer, designer, conductor, singers and orchestra who were not Mozart and who, in the decision about dating, had boldly asserted that they were not. It was theirs too.

And it was anyone's who could get a ticket – '*my* Mozart'.

The long detour lands us back with Moule's wonderfully pregnant phrase 'continuities which make the hermeneutic task (the job of interpreting) possible': but with a new respect for the scrapes and complexities of the process which makes us underline the word *hermeneutic*. There's the rub. Continuity, yes. Without it the cunningly creative tension would break. But because it is by means of hermeneutic, of more or less apt interpretation worked out under all sorts of pressures of time, continuity with whom and with what exactly?

To focus on Jesus again. Any sense of his presence will draw deeply on the New Testament records and appeal to them for its authentication. And Jesus there, in that ultimate source and court of appeal, is always 'according to . . .' someone or other, some interpreter or other who makes the continuity possible. If I take a bit from one interpreter and a bit from another, as churchgoers commonly do in forming their picture of the Jesus who is present to them (*my* Jesus), I will not apparently have got further back to the historical Jesus but will have added yet another interpretation to keep the pot a-bojling. In this process, moving in both senses, the historical Jesus has diffused himself and disappeared into that communion with his followers or participants where the historical quest for him slows to a halt. But suppose the quest for him succeeds. One thing is certain about what is then found. It is, whatever else, a man nourished by the past, a head and heart full of Old Testament words and themes so that to understand him we would have to go back past him into that past which he lived from and interpreted.

As on a bad old radio set, it will never be one voice only that we hear, nor will it be possible indisputably to distinguish one voice from another: not with Mozart's whose autograph scores we have, still less with Jesus whose we don't. Forward from the point in time occupied by the figure in the past who interests us, in the space between him and us, is the many-stranded line of intermediary interpreters. They make a difference. Back from him is the long line of tradition which he inherited, which makes every genius and every apostle so very derivative a figure, so very deeply and widely indebted to the past which has nourished and forms him in his digestive interpretation of it. That makes a difference too. Not only is the figure whom we seek inextricably an interpreted person, he is himself an interpreter. Our search for him is always and properly slipping back into his past and forward into his future: and in such a continuum of tangled influences and interpretations, he lives, moves and has his being. That is how historical study goes. Like Ibsen's Peer Gynt we peel the onion hoping to find an inner core of pure meaning or unadulterated gospel. But there is only peel and the meaning, if any, is in the peeling. Such a process does not seem at all likely to provide the sort of solid plinth needed for the erection of any permanently stable and ever-valid christology, for the very liveliness and sensitivity of the interpretative historical method militates against the possibility of making any figure in the past an isolable, rock-like, sharp-edged ultimate referent in this way – which is just what Christians usually try to do with Christ. It does *not* mean that he is inaccessible, that we cannot be present to him or he to us. It means that we can never be as certain that it is he alone and no other who is involved as we Christians have got used to thinking – a failure to isolate him which no amount of 'believing' that it is he and no other will fill.

This tortuous, but I hope not wayward or unintelligible road, has consequences for the doctrine of Christ which can be faced positively by returning to two aspects of it which we glimpsed ahead on setting out: catholicism and the Holy Spirit.

Catholicism – because the appeal to Christ isolated and alone is simply forbidden us by the evidence having rubbed our noses in the old churchyard truth that time is an ever-rolling stream. Christ, historically in that continuum and doctrinally too if we grasp the doctrine of incarnation, is present to us inseparable from those to whom he gave himself and who digested him into their own systems, such as the Paul for whom to live was Christ. He was not isolated and is not isolable. He is in a *communio sanctorum* in which the New Testament writers are eminent but far from alone. And every Christian conversion is a double affair, of a person into Christ and of Christ into that person, which leaves nothing quite the same. It is worth recalling that Eliot at Little Gidding was not convinced of only one figure, Christ, being present though past, but of many – some of them apparently from the England of the seventeenth century.

The Holy Spirit – because here we have something of a history of inspiration, of dead tradition ever being raised to new life in history, of Augustine's beauty so old and so new. Of this vivifying interaction of spirit and time, John's gospel speaks. It comes nearest to christomonism of all the New Testament writers, and his 'I am' sayings are grist to the mills of the most thorough-going contemporary christocentrics. But with a characteristic tip of emphasis he corrects himself. The Spirit will take up the future when Christ is gone, bringing the past to present remembrance and life (14.25) and speaking things that he did not say but belong to him, in continuities which make that interpretative task possible.

The way in which Christ is present fits with the myth of incarnation so long as incarnation is seen in the thorough-going and unexclusive way which is demanded both by its own energy and by historical criticism. It has to be thorough-going because only so can it maintain the Christian claim to be a thoroughly historical religion which at no point calls on the historian to down tools; and only so can it avoid the error of making Christ something other than entirely human at some crucial point. It has to be unexclusive because only so can it maintain Christianity's claim to be a universal religion; and because acknowledging anyone's humanity, in the deep and existential way which is needed if the acknowledgement is to be more than formal, entails the refusal of imagining oneself or anyone else to have the immunity to criticism of a privileged special case. It is clear enough that what passes for orthodoxy often refuses both these conditions and holds their opposites. Christ is a uniquely special case because his is a divinity 'which in your case you do not have'. So he becomes the ideal focus or reflection of a world-shy community which talks *de haut en bas* when it feels called upon to reflect on wordly-goings on and more ordinarily enjoys the sense of being closer to Christ than the numerous non-members – who are welcome to join their ranks if they will share their ideal but are otherwise something of a race apart.

The distortion which gives rise to such attitudes is a subtle one which is entitled to the sympathy of anybody with a deep-seated conviction that, while he is human, one of the boys or girls of whom not too much should be expected and a great deal excused, he is by some modest measurement a little more enlightened or endearing than his fellows and entitled to special consideration. If that includes, as is likely, everybody, it is obviously not an inclusive attitude or a saving one. It is common in the superficial sense of being widely held, but not in the deeper sense of living as a creature among creatures in 'the house of the God of life'. The uniqueness of Christ, to be saving and universal, must have this second kind of commonness. And it does have it, whether we contemplate it in its mythical form of divine power and privilege renounced for the world's sake (the opposite of the world well lost for privilege and power's sake), or in its historical form of the man who found community amongst acknowledged sinners and excommunication from the *beati possidentes* of religious rectitude. And if *their* subsequent achievement has been to erect, in christological dogma, the most magnificent tomb ever loaded on a murdered prophet, their building still bears witness to the power of self-denial (more modestly, of other interests) which they could not accommodate. 'Thy glory is declared, even in that which denies Thee . . . their denial is never complete.'[12] So there must also be an end of the bilious pleasures of knocking the establishment which is the ultimate triumph of the we/them mentality, mythically fostered by Satan as 'accuser of the brethren'. In the end we are knocking ourselves as people who can neither accommodate the glory which breaks from the renunciation of glory for love of the common, nor fail to respond and witness to it in some way or other. From this penitential point, as from no other, we can set out to discover traces of its activity in the common human world. In that sense the rest of this book will be a sort of natural theology. But it will not, if possible, be natural theology of the sort which discredits itself by lending a hand to sectional interest. In concerning itself, however episodically, with other interests, it will attempt to go on as it began and to discover divinity giving itself away 'at the centre of life'.

5

The Individual Christian

In the latter years of his life, Soren Kierkegaard used to spend Sunday mornings sitting ostentatiously in the window of his club reading the newspaper. It was his way of setting a religious example to the public, a prophetic sign in the tradition of Jeremiah walking about Jerusalem with a yoke round his neck or Hosea's marriage to a whore, meant to make clear in an action louder than words what the prophet saw to be the truth of things. In his own individual person he dramatized his doctrine. Kierkegaard had always done that. These Sunday mornings were little climaxes of a life spent attacking the Christian collective, 'Christendom', its sterility and hypocrisy. In his last journals he wrote that genuine Christianity 'consists of the demand to dare as a single person to have to do with God. We men reply, Let us unite to worship God; the more we are, the happier, the truer and the more we shall please God.' The real content of this was, 'Let us rebel against God, let us see that we are strong in the face of God.'[1] So the real venture of Christianity 'which needs the courage of despair and the greatest of all efforts' was evaded. That venture was something that men and women had to undertake on their own, but it was found that 'the more we are together, the happier we shall be'.

At a time when ecumenism and eucharistic or biblical fellowship use up so much religious energy it takes a little time to realize the obvious, if necessarily exaggerated,[2] truth of what Kierkegaard was saying. The whole Christian tradition, which has the character of a corporate possession like a National Gallery, owes virtually everything to the creativity of individual encounters with the divine, aside from the collective and usually against its grain. The major New Testament writings come from a time before the full establishment of the Christian collective, when small churches could support individual leaders who were not slow to contradict other ones or recast their ideas drastically. Kierkegaard, like so many other critics, was able to appeal to the New Testament against the church. From Moses through the prophets and Job, to the lonely figure of Paul who made a theological point of his independence of the apostolic establishment at Jerusalem (Galatians 1), and on to Martin Luther and John Henry Newman and Dietrich Bonhoeffer, the work which gives religion its vitality and life has been done by people on their own – and with some of the isolation coming from the distrust and uncomprehending fear of the leaders of the collective. Jesus remarked that such prophets are customarily killed by one generation and then get monuments built over them in the next. The Bible is a cemetery containing many such tombs. Perhaps this is because the collective is a slow beast in getting round to things, in theology as in art and letters often taking more than an innovator's life-time to understand what he was at. Perhaps darker and more dreadful forces hamper it, as Kierkegaard thought. Anyhow, it is clear enough that in creativity, however much is owed to the collective, everything turns on the individual confronting the big things afresh. Nor is this only so with the big figures, the genius and the apostle. The banalities of life have not happened until they have happened to oneself. Birth, love and death: these are things a person goes through on his own or not at all. Friends can only help from a distance and perhaps best by supportive silence. And these are the points of encounter with God *par excellence*. Kierkegaard seems to have been right. It is as single persons that we have to do with God. The creativity which Jung saw as so essential to religion's survival is a solitary business at its crucial point, which in Christianity is occupied by the cross, where solitariness achieves its definitive symbol and historical instance in the person cut off from divine-human community – and where that community begins again. Once more we must beware of the quasi-objective approach which sees it as 'once, only once' in the sense of concealing a heartfelt wish that this sort of thing need not, must not, happen again elsewhere, that we are let off it because it was an objectively unique occurrence. Not only will historical criticism undermine it; the theology of Paul and others insists that people become Christians, and so a church exists, precisely by squeezing through this gate: so narrow that it only takes one at a time at the most.

The individual matters in point of universal fact. There is a basic aloneness about a human being which is brought home in the fundamental realization that he is neither anybody else nor God. But this frighteningly ascetic perception leads to another which is more cheerful. The individual matters in point of the strategy of creativity. Once freed from the apron-strings, he is able to make contributions to the general benefit which were not possible before. Every point of transition in the process of his growing makes this clear. His range of interests increases and clarifies along with the 'individuation' which increases and clarifies his unique character. In particular, while belonging to a collective, like a church, he comes to belong more and more to other things as well – his family, friends, desk, game, landscape and God. This means that by never being entirely a churchman, he does the kind of cross-fertilizing, the bringing together of things otherwise apart, which is as basic to making a joke with vitality as a vital religion – syncretism and miscegenation are dirty words in sterile places. The individual is the only place, we might say, at which the church loves its enemies or at least its rivals, those other forms of life which have claims on a person's time. And it is not exactly love in a full sense when these things are taken over and subsumed under the church as Christian families, Christian drama and so on. If the church does not grudge or discourage this, it has, more or less gladly, to acknowledge something of the importance of disloyalty which Graham Greene wrote of in a letter where the references to the state are applicable to the church too:[3]

> You remember Tom Paine's apothegm, 'we must take care to guard even our enemies against injustice', and it is here that the writer has great opportunities and greater obligations than the chemist or the estate agent. . . . Now the State is invariably ready to confuse, like a schoolmaster, justice with retribution, and isn't it possibly the storyteller's task to act as the devil's advocate, to elicit sympathy and a measure of understanding for those outside State Sympathy? . . . It has always been in the interest of the State to poison the psychological wells, to restrict human sympathy, to encourage catcalls – Galilean, Papist, Crophead, Fascist, Bolshevik. . . I would emphasize once again the importance, the virtue of disloyalty. Loyalty confines us to accepted opinions: loyalty forbids us to comprehend sympathetically our dissident fellows; but disloyalty encourages us to roam experimentally through any human mind, it gives to the novelist the extra dimension of sympathy.

Greene is using disloyalty there, in the unbuttoned liberty to exaggerate of private correspondence, to talk of an over-riding loyalty to the love of neighbour as a creative force over the head of loyalty to the collective which is a conservative force. The church is a collective with a difference; according to an idealistic *mot* of Archbishop William Temple's, the only institution which exists solely for the sake of those who do not belong to it. At a rather more humdrum level it is an institution which stands under the commandment to love neighbours with a deliberate refusal to restrict that vast field, and so an institution which cannot expect its members to have a great deal of time to spend on maintaining itself.

This reflection could cast a cheerful light on something which can be confusing and irritating. Modern religious man, Karl Rahner has noticed,[4] wills to be a heretic within the church. He wills to be a heretic because he cannot honestly understand in his head and heart all that the church holds necessary to salvation, and so it follows that he cannot, in the deep religious sense which is presumably meant, commit himself to it all. He wills to be in the church because he is not romantically carried away by his

own deep convictions or self-righteously persuaded of their
incorrigible rightness. He wants to belong to a community
where they can be held in place and corrected. So he
relativizes the church by his refusal to abase himself before
all its dogmas, whether they mean anything to him or not,
his reserving of the right to ask questions. And he
relativizes himself in the same way. The relativizing is not
only a playing down, although that is certainly and
necessarily entailed. It is a playing down in order to bring
together two things in the sort of tension and equal
dialogue which is necessary to creativity and its concomitant
loving. 'Only connect . . .' And connections of the sort
which are vital to the life of religion can only be made
by such disloyal-cum-loyal, heretical-cum-ecclesiastical
individuals. It is the relativizing which they apply to
themselves, the institutions they belong to and their
neighbours which brings them all together in a sharing of
the world which can be constructive. Myth and fact, the
church's dream-world and the politician's material world,
the necessity of being oneself and the necessity of
belonging, the relative and the absolute: they can only get
to speaking with one another through the endurance of
the individual who will not let either go. Within the
collective the wheels go round and round, but move
nothing outside. Within the individual who neither sells
out nor makes a unilateral declaration of independence
they have to interact. But before looking at some instances
of that interaction on which so much depends, it is
necessary to say a little more about the curious situation
of the person who makes them because it is determinative
of the way he does so.

Suppose he is asked the question 'Are you a Christian?'
The more superficial its intention, the easier it is to answer.
There is little to worry about if it comes from a sociologist
in Western Europe seeking to determine the number of
people in a population who have been baptized. There
may be very slightly more to worry about if the sociologist
is doing the more difficult job of determining how many
people go to church on Sunday more often than not, or

if the vicar is drawing up a mailing list of people who would show their interest in the church by coming to some of its functions and giving money to it. Then the question of some deeper and more personal allegiance begins to obtrude. There is everything to worry about if the question is aimed deeply enough to have some of the force which drove William Cowper into pathological depression: 'Are you one of God's elect and redeemed, witnessed so in your inmost conviction and outward works, or an eternally damned reprobate?' It would not be put so sharply nowadays, but by reaching below formalities and debating points it prods seriously at a religious nerve and is not answered by a faultless record of almsgiving or church attendance, nor even by the cherished memory of a heart-warming experience in the course of an evangelistic campaign. At this point the question really matters and needs to be handled with the greatest delicacy and aplomb because it can be devilishy improper if used to exclude or torment: whether by one person of another or by one person of himself. 'At this searching, radical level are you a Christian?' The sort of answer required needs to be nothing less than fully theological and fully personal, and will lay bare the mechanics by which Christian discipleship gears into life.

According to the gospels, Jesus was asked at his trial if he was the Christ. Mark says that he answered 'I am', the other three that he said something like 'that is what you say, those are your words'. The back-to-you parrying of these later editorial versions is deliberate enough to invite considered reflection. According to a very sensible Jewish tradition a man was not allowed to proclaim himself the Christ or Messiah. That was to be done by God's evident favour towards him and the perceptive witness of his fellow men. If something of this sort informs the later versions, there is an obvious parallel with the person asked if he is a Christian. Like master, like disciple: an evasive answer has to be returned because the definitive answer is not his to give. It lies with God and his neighbours. His refusal or renunciation of it is a silence of faith in them, a waiting upon them and a leaving of the initiative to them, which is more than defensive modesty. It is love expressing itself out of a very tight corner. It is all of a piece with the fundamental Christianity of working out the commandment to love God and neighbour, and its saving power. A person is rescued from the self-centred solipsism of worrying 'am I a Christian?' by the gospel which says that he must lose his life – at its centre, and not in a few 'charitable' or institutionally obedient acts – for God and neighbour if he would really find it. To put it very sharply, it is only the Christian who does not much care whether he is one who is one: necessarily so if love of God and neighbour is what it is all about.

It is not possible to forget, or lose, oneself by a trick of self-induced amnesia: that is the famous ethical bind of 'he's trying to be the humblest man in Ireland'. It happens rather when a man chases a woman or loses his careful temper, oblivious of the startling or silly figure he cuts in public; when he forgets his lunch because he is making dovetail joints or a sandcastle. When things like that are going on, his posture tells other people that his life, all his physical and mental powers, are absorbed in something other than himself. In just this sense the true Christian's life is 'hid with Christ in God', and the answer to the daunting question is hid there, too. It is also hidden in his neighbours. According to the parable of the sheep and the goats in Matthew 25.31–46, the vindication of the sheep came to them as a complete surprise. They were, literally, the last people to know about it. It had long since gone out of their control and into the contributions they made to the well-being of others, and in the extensive meanwhile any guesses of their own about their religious standing would have been beside the determinative point.

The points of interaction which go to make it must have the same pattern, character or family likeness. Instead of self-proclamation and preservation they have to be creative ways of getting lost if they really gear in. It was for failing along these lines with its myth that Jung rebuked the church and warned it of imminent death. He pointed to the mystics as a way forward. Without doubt they are classic instances of the way of life we are exploring, and as such attract such sensitively serious *aficionados* of religion as Charles Williams and T. S. Eliot, as well as a host of less articulate people. But though I rarely read them without being stimulated and illuminated, I am not a mystical enough character to do them anything like the justice done by others whose work is available. Besides, the points of interaction I am looking for are more obviously commonplace ('obviously' because so many mystics have a more commonplace religion than most clergymen or theologians) and accessible to a wider, because less literate, public. The first is happy and the second gloomy.

Christmas Fathers

At Christmas the individual Christian annually finds himself in the unusually pleasant situation of having his lives at home, at work and in church coming neatly together. The same greetings, images and attitudes are required in them all. Nearly everybody who does not have a clear alternative religious allegiance celebrates this Christian festival somehow, and a surprising number by going to church. If Jung was pointing in the right direction, all this could well be because a myth is working: either as it is, or in a modern development, or both.

First, the church's old story as it is works with very little assistance in what a modernist might call the right direction, and even seems to get through a great deal of deliberate mock-mediaeval nonsense with an élan which leaves questions of fact and fiction standing – and, more critically, outstanding. At one end it is as homely as can be, with the basic human unit of man, woman and child at the centre. At the other end it is fantastic, speculative, awesome. 'Away in a manger', Christmas presents, and the pleasures of the table have as secure a place in it as the reading of John, chapter 1, and the attempts by clergymen to expound the doctrine of the incarnation. None of these really suffices on its own – not even the doctrine of the incarnation, which is surely in any case understood by very few in the pulpit or the congregation *as a doctrine*, if as such it is intelligible at all. The whole

business, from the big stores to the altar, is itself an
incarnation for a religion usually far too preoccupied with
words, and it works unstoppably. In such a range there
is something for everybody. And if there is a centre it is
in a birth, which means something to everybody. To be
present at a birth, as fathers are nowadays invited to be,
is to take part in an efficacious ritual which can remind
a Christian of the ritual at the altar while being, at the
level of obviousness anyhow, more gripping and impressive.
Round the white bed and the white-shirted mother gather
the intermediary figures of doctor and nurses vested in
green. Whatever the reason, and it is probably quite
practical, the colours tell symbolically. The pace of labour
quickens and concentration tightens to an alarming pitch.
Quite suddenly, amid all the white and the green
surrounding it, come the bright colours of life: red, lots
of red, and yellows and blues – a splash of primary
colours and the primal sounds of crying, sighs of relief,
congratulation. What happens many times a day in a
modern hospital is about the same thing as is celebrated
in church more politely and less nerve-rackingly. With
such associations, no wonder the gospel works, because
the old tale is in close touch with reality.

Secondly, Christmas has been widely and popularly
developed in myth: particularly that part of it which might
seem to have been left out so far – Christmas as the
presence of God in the world. Father Christmas comes on
to the scene. In origin he is a folk-figure of northern
mythology. An old pagan elf, his head wreathed in holly
and mistletoe, he brought the yule log and the steaming
bowl. So, but younger, he appears in Dickens' *A Christmas
Carol* as the spirit of Christmas present, dressed in green,
holding a flaming torch and surrounded by heaps of food
and drink. He secured his place in unofficial Christian
celebration by being absorbed into St Nicholas and by
going to America, whence he returned as the figure known
in England today, dressed in red on his reindeer sleigh
with his sack of toys. As such he comes annually to the
serious Christian as one whom it would be unnecessarily
severe to exclude and yet presenting an uncomfortable

problem. The Christian is supposed to believe in a father-god in heaven. As we have seen, he does so with an embarrassed tenuousness betrayed in his refusal to be literal and call him the father in the sky. He believes, more strongly, that whatever this divinity's home ground (which is scarcely the phrase anyhow), he has made himself accessible in our world by means of a strange birth and a life spent in gifts of grace to those who could accept them as children, the 'little ones' whose lives he cheered with effective traces of his elusive presence. Are such beliefs mocked, all too pointedly, or somehow confirmed by Father Christmas? He is another embodiment of the religious imagination with precisely the features which theologians and secularists mock in the popular Christian version: old, benign and airborne. He squeezes down the chimney like a baby down the birth passage, to come into ordinary rooms and distribute presents. He is gone before anyone sees him. As a matter of fact mothers and fathers do the solid bit of his business, the providential giving, for him and for their children and one another:

> a Divinity so odd
> He lets the Adam whom He made
> Perform the Acts of God.[5]

Such considerations put us on ground no less dangerous for being charming. We are involved in a *scherzo* which, as often in such symphonic movements, edges on the menacing. It could be the foolishness of God which is wiser than our attempts at statesmanship. But when religion gets out of the hands of its officials and flourishes in shops and houses, they are likely to feel that, though they hoped for something like this to happen, it was not exactly this that they had in mind. They divert attention from Christmas trees and Father Christmas and fix it on the serious, the 'historical' centre which is the incarnation of God in Jesus Christ. The absurdly fanciful and indulgent nature of Father Christmas invites sympathy for such efforts from any serious Christian person. But then his centre is also wrapped in imaginative story, which has to be recognized as such. And the wrapping is apparently not exactly accidental or dispensable for, whatever the centre is, mythical tales of some kind seem to be needed to present it. Besides which, an unwrapped present is immediately recognized as short on tender loving care. When the myth of Father Christmas is played against the myth of divine incarnation, we are made conscious that it is kinds of myth, in the first instance, that we are dealing with. Hence the sense of danger and alarm. But the next, the very important, question is why these two myths are there for us to deal with at all. The answer lies in that apprehension of giving as the spiritual centre of life which becomes ordinarily real at historical moments: at the moment when the stockings are filled, the moment of the Last Supper and the moments of the events which followed that, the moment of sending a Christmas card to someone who was nearly forgotten, and thousands of other such moments. Nothing but myth of some kind or other would serve both to attract our jaded attention into action and to get the action done in the celebratory-cum-inevitable spirit which is so much more appropriate to it than a grim obedience to a moral imperative on which we congratulate ourselves. It becomes a laughably small contribution ('Oh, not at all. It's really nothing') set in the majestic and highly coloured frame which both commands it and makes it good without pomposity or solipsism. Both our myths reach the point of fulfilment, without which they are pointlessly tall stories, when someone gives something to somebody else and it is given and taken as an instance of the gift of self which makes selfhood. That is, as far as Christians know, God.

Old Mortality

At the other end of the human scenario from birth and celebration are death and mourning. It is the same with the gospel story of Jesus which churchgoing Christians hear told and retold with the church's sacred-cum-secular year – but adding something more. Resurrection follows in the gospel narratives, numerous Sundays after Trinity or after Pentecost in the year. It is very hard to say what this 'something more' is: hard for the careful biblical scholar to say what is meant by Jesus' resurrection in view of the strikingly diverse versions of it and its consequences in the New Testament, hard for the careful Christian to find out how it can be believed and lived. It seems to be like an algebraic symbol outside the bracket which transforms the value of everything inside it in its terms: but we know only the things inside the bracket. Putting it another way, 'something more' is not an apt phrase because it suggests something gratuitously tacked on, whereas people who go to church (far less of them at Easter than at Christmas) are likely to be told that this is half the truth intended at most. There is no resurrection without death; the new life comes out of the old in some sort of continuity as well as out of the end of the old in discontinuity. It is not just a reversal. It is something of a consequence too. The practical result of this doctrinal see-sawing is that we are allowed, and possibly even obliged in Christian and in ordinary terms, to start where we are by grasping the certainty of death.

It is difficult to know whether we are well or badly placed at the present time to do this. It has been said *ad nauseam* that death receives at our hands the sort of shabby treatment, as of an embarrassingly dirty and ill-behaved relation, which sex got from our grandparents. There is, or at least until recently has been, a good deal in this complaint. The stark emphasis on mortality of the old Anglican funeral service seems to have struck its revisers as too dour, but they have been far outdone in this line by the famous activities of American morticians and the consensus among doctors and the public that dying should be done in the seclusion of hospital. There has undoubtedly been some fudging of the great issue which leaves the individual unhelped in his task of confronting it face to face. But he is helped by an opposite, if equally suspect, movement. Driven out of the ordinary domestic and ecclesiastical way of things, the old man returns in lurid vigour on to cinema and television screens. People queued for *Jaws* and the spate of death-and-disaster films which followed: possibly not simply out of ghoulishness but as a way of getting to terms with the majestic fact when other ways are denied them. Why do people enjoy this sort of thing enough to stand in the cold and pay for it? On a more august and respectable level, why go to Bach's St Matthew Passion, or the great tragedies which end with corpses on the stage, or even the Christian death-sacrament of Holy Communion, and come away feeling better? From Aristotle onwards the question has been canvassed and answered, and the most convincing answer seems to be that it is the unathletic person's equivalent of rock-climbing or solo ocean racing; that he feels better for having faced the worst and that he comes out of it with a renewed sense of value and preciousness. There is indeed a quite ordinary sense in which anybody's death, actual or foreseen as bound to happen, sharpens the other people's sense of their worth: the worth of the deceased and of those still left in public. Hence not only the funeral eulogy but also much silent evaluative meditation surrounding every death.

This can be taken further into a particularly modern and new consciousness – of the death, some day, of the world. Cosmologists assure us that this will happen. It is a jolt to ordinary rationalism, which is usually based on the notion that things will carry on much as now for ever, and so could spark off two unreasonable reactions. The first is cynicism, but it requires a bleak heroism or a terrified inertia of which not many people are ordinarily capable for long. The second is love, in the sense that what is mortal ought, as with human beings, to be all the more urgently cared for in the finite period when caring is possible. This second reaction is boosted by another new consciousness about our planet: that our ransacking and spoiling of it could kill it before the bigger forces have their chance. It has certainly led to a more affectionate and cherishing attitude to it, an attitude which takes us back to some of those basic things of religion which Christianity has too long left in a pagan past – particularly the idea that earth is our mother, that the sea is something more than a great waste, larder or dump but has a being of its own. Wordsworth tried to bring back to a materialistic Christian world such a consciousness of nature and the spirituality of matter in a sonnet of 1807:

The world is too much with us; late and soon,
Getting and spending, we lay waste our powers:
Little we see in nature that is ours;
We have given our hearts away, a sordid boon!
The sea that bares her bosom to the moon;
The winds that will be howling at all hours,
And are up-gathered now like sleeping flowers;
For this, for everything, we are out of tune;
It moves us not – Great God! I'd rather be
A pagan suckled in a creed outworn;
So might I, standing on this pleasant lea,
Have glimpses that would make me less forlorn;
Have sight of Proteus rising from the sea;
Or hear old Triton blow his wreathed horn.

It does move us rather more in an ecologically-conscious time, and the scientists' facts and predictive figures have put us more in tune. The myth of the earth is coming back because it is functionally and responsibly necessary: necessary, we could say, to our salvation if we use that big religious word in the secular sense which it demands. It is a godsend to a religion in need of new myths but not, one hopes, ready to fall for any old myths, but only those which do justice to the created order as science describes it and as we live in it. We have here a way of describing the place we live in which is far more wholesomely to the point than the recent revival of exorcism. It comes through scientific observation rather than defying it or capitalizing on its gaps. It points towards a genuine love of the place, based on the finding that as creatures we are more part of it than we supposed. The creaturely love of the relative becomes our religious duty, not least when the relatives are found to be the animals: as Darwin, so shockingly to our religious forebears, announced. We have more neighbours than theology has traditionally supposed.

It is worth noticing that we have been introduced to them by a sort of revival of paganism as well as by the more respectable men in white coats. This goes against the grain of traditional Christianity, which has been careful either to reject paganism or to borrow from it very surreptitiously indeed. Judaism and Christianity both established and re-established themselves by exclusive distinction from the sacred woods and rivers, the fertility rites and nature-ceremonies which proliferated in the surrounding world. But once they have gone or been driven into corners, the situation is different. Their worst features – demonology, positivism of the *Volk* or race, ritual murder – can break cover and attack all the more effectively people whose unfamiliarity with them makes discrimination weak or impossible. Their best features – reverence for life as an organic bundle or totality, the sense of natural wonder and of God in nature – can by their absence impoverish religion into a high-minded sectarianism which easily falls prey to Philistine materialism. Hence the surreptitious and random borrowing, not just at Christmas but also at Easter with its eggs and daffodils. Hence Wordsworth's plea. Over and above all this, however, the Christian is driven this way, as we have seen, by the energy of a gospel about the descent of the divine into the secular, put in a myth which arguably owes something to the drama of the dying and rising God of natural mysteries.[6] It is far from implying unreflective assent to everything in natural life, but it commands an inclusive evaluation of everything in natural life in its terms. 'Finally, brethren, whatsoever things are true, whatsoever things are honourable, whatsoever things are just, whatsoever things are pure, whatsoever things are lovely, whatsoever things are of good report: if there be any virtue, and if there be any praise, think on these things' (Philippians 4.8). If it is not, as a few scholars guess, Paul who speaks but, as they allow, a close disciple of his, it is striking that a strong theological line which began with stringent world denial should move into such delicately generous assent – something, perhaps, of a resurrection after crucifixion.

To get a meaning out of death has meant going through three movements. First it was necessary to cut free from the myths: to scrap those of the mortician's parlour because they are too cheap, to postpone the grand Christian one of resurrection because it is only really intelligible at a later stage. The unadorned fact has to be faced as a sheer certainty. Finally, through this process of losing a new meaning and value can come about. So the body, *any* body, is raised to a level of spirituality which returns us to a sense of its resurrection. The old myth can mean something after all. It is reduced, it is even secularized, but it is something. And with myths as with people it is better to be thinner and integrated than fat and worried.

Time

The same series of movements can be applied to time. Here a story will be a relief from the abstracting of attitudes into concepts. In *Der Rosenkavalier*[7] the drama turns on love accepting time and becoming more itself by doing so. The aging Feldmarschallin has a young lover Oktavian who thinks romantically that the intensity of their affair makes it permanent and even eternal. But she, the Feldmarschallin, has learned otherwise in the very solitary and hard-eyed discipline of the middle-aged woman looking into the mirror. Then, quite suddenly, time, which had not seemed to matter before, is seen to be trickling through everything:

> And between me and you,
> There too it flows, soundless like an hourglass.

The immediate reaction is to get up and stop all the clocks. But then comes the turning point:

> Nevertheless we are not to shrink from it,
> For it too is a creature of the Father who created us all.

It is a turning point that we have seen before, the discovery of a shared world of relativity as all that we have. It can be the actualizing in individual life of the great Christian myth of the divine being who saves mortal beings by descending into their world of irrevocable time and certain death. It is a turning point, although dreaded as an end, because love is the other side of it: again, reduced and relativized, but saving. The Feldmarschallin gives Oktavian the silver rose, the betrothal gift from her grotesque cousin Baron Ochs, to take to the young Sophie Faninal. She makes him the *Rosenkavalier*, knowing that this meeting with Sophie will result in a new love for him which will take him away from her as well as Ochs. She leaves too, also for love on the other side of this little death. First she will go to church to pray; that is, to give God the love due to him from his creatures. Then she will go to supper with her old uncle Greifenau, 'because it pleases the old man', that is for one creature to give to another, an elderly relation, the love due from one to another. 'You shall love the Lord your God . . . and your neighbour as yourself.' Time, accepted, brings her nearer to both.

That is, as it always has been, Christianity. It is something to be done within the constraints, even by means of the constraints, of any particular time. 'You shall love your crooked neighbour with your crooked heart.'[8] The subjection of traditional Christianity to the constraints of the present day, the old inescapable banalities of the churchyard and the new methods of critical analysis, cannot avoid reducing it and smudging the lines between it and ordinary human experience. But just those things, the comparative smallness and the ordinariness, leave the business of being a Christian as something which can be done and has to be done.

Beauty and the Beast

This last topic will serve to repeat and fasten the pattern of the previous investigations. The relation of Christianity to beauty is a neglected topic: understandably, because the Christian religion, like its parent Judaism, contains an irreducible element of Puritanism. Paul stood in a majestic tradition when he launched his blitz on the grounds for human boasting and glory, making a positive theological point of this own inelegant speaking and the lack of sophistication among his hearers. Just as the prophets of old had called their people to a naked encounter with God in the desert and in judgment, so Paul summoned his contemporaries to find him in the nothingness of the cross. On 10 July 1855 Soren Kierkegaard made an entry in his journal under the title *To love God – or to love ugliness*. It is immediately clear that he did not regard these two as alternatives but as allies:

> To love ugliness – yes, quite right! For if I am, as indeed I am, flesh and blood, a being of senses, an animal creation, then 'spirit' is the most terrible thing for me, terrible as death, and to love spirit is the most terrible thing of all. So too Christianity understands it, it teaches that to love God means to die, to die to the world, the worst of all torments – blessed is he who is not offended.
>
> That is why, in times when Christianity was taken seriously, those who took it seriously made use of a death's head for their contemplation. Of course one cannot say that the spirit is like a death's head, for the spirit is not like any object of the senses. But a death's head was the most significant symbol.[9]

What chance has beauty under the hammer of such penitential doctrine? Even if we aim off a little for Kierkegaard's dogged counter-suggestibility, his point sticks. The primal roots of Christianity are not in the artistic triumphs of the prosperous city, but among people living in the wilderness and in tents – neither of which is promising material for the development of the fine arts. Our religion begins with the word in the desert, the death outside the city. It is the function of the prophet to remind us of that – in season and out.

The reminder could hardly be more unwelcome and unseasonable than it is now, as enterprising theologians try to claim friends for their cause from among the painters, poets and musicians. This projected alliance entails the framing of a theology of beauty. But we may not properly go about making it with our ears stopped against the prophetic summons or our eyes shut (in this century of all times) against the death's head. Our situation is grave. On one flank we are assailed by a God who jealously refuses to be associated with any graven image or the likeness of anything in land, air or sea; on the other by ugliness, the brute fact. And Kierkegaard is right: these two, spirit and death's head, will join forces to harass anyone who tries to leave them out in order to cultivate beauty in the dilettante's no-man's-land. A proper Christian theology of beauty will follow Beauty's way with the Beast

in the fairy tale – and embrace that which repels it. There
is a place for beauty in Christianity, a firm place, but on
the strict condition that it itself allows place for its two
disturbers – God and ugliness.

Before attempting to locate it, we may reflect that we
would be in just the same predicament if we were going
about the more usual business of making Christian ethics.
There again we would not be allowed to preoccupy
ourselves simply with good conduct without continual
attention to the two things which put it in question: evil,
and the God whose ways are so unlike ours that we
should hesitate to stick our notions of good conduct on
to him. (Is it not, after all, his presence which rubs our
noses in the mystery of evil?) When the ethical man, all
unsuspecting, steps into Christianity he, like the aesthete,
is instantly subjected to a co-ordinated attack on both
flanks. The gospel of forgiveness and the cross raises the
alarm: the God who escapes categories of good ethics by
transcending them has got in league with the sinners who
flout and fall short of them. God's hand is nailed to the
cross. And that leaves the ethical man's centre, his moral
discrimination and his practice of virtue, confused and
isolated. No wonder that he catches, if he is honest, a
whiff of the demonic in such a strategy. If he is to carry
on in the face of this and do Christian ethics he will have
to engage with those two shockingly allied forces.
Forgiveness, which has brought them together, has made
his strong centre, his righteousness, into the place where
the issue will not be decided.

The Christian must think about beauty without trying
to shield his meditation from God or from ugliness. More,
he has to heed the command to love his enemies – and
who are they but the ones who threaten to destroy what
he cherishes? He will not achieve that without the climbing-
down, the renunciation and loss, through which the gospel
promises life and gain. Now he comes near to the centre
of the matter, and as he does so he follows apostolic
example by referring himself, not to concepts, but to the
mythical story, cutting into brutal history, which lies
behind this whole investigation.

Who subsisting in the form of God
Did not deem equality with God
Something to be grasped,
But emptied himself
Taking the form of a slave.

And being as men are
And in fashion found as a man,
He was humbler yet,
Being obedient to death,
Even death on a cross.

Therefore God raised him high,
And gave him the name above names,
So that all beings
In the heavens, and on earth, and in the deep,
Should bend the knee at the name of Jesus
And that every tongue should acclaim
Jesus Christ as Lord
To the glory of God the Father. (Philippians 2)

The word *morphe*, form, meaning subsistence expressed in shape, suggests an aesthetic interpretation. So here is a story in which myth assists history to embrace the highest and most serene beauty (the form of God) and the most abysmal and insecure ugliness (the form of a slave). Worse, we are presented with a descent into utter formlessness, for even ugliness has shapes – but death dissolves them. Then comes the birth of a new form of beauty out of the abyss: this same being, exalted, adored and home again 'to the glory of God'. The descent of pure form and beauty into its opposite so happens that it emerges in a form whose purity and serenity no longer cut it off from the disgusting features of our lives.

This type of pattern can be recognized in countless instances. It is older than Christianity.

Without beauty, without majesty (we saw him)
And no beauty that we should desire him . . .
And as one from whom men hide their faces
He was despised and we esteemed him not.

Yet:

After all his pains he shall be bathed in light,
After his disgrace he shall be fully vindicated,

By his sufferings shall my servant make many good. (Isaiah . 53).

Here are two further examples of it: one which refers to art and one which refers to ethics.

Rembrandt painted plain middle-aged people without any clothes on as a counterblast to the Renaissance nude. He also did an etching of the Good Samaritan. An unpleasant and prominent feature of it is a dog squatting in the foreground and defaecating. Sir Kenneth Clark says this about it:

> It is Rembrandt's dogmatic sermon against the frivolity of elegance. The forms are not simply ungraceful; they are reduced to clouts and clods. The figures hang from one another like a string of potatoes, and their sequence of lumpish shapes comes most sharply into focus with the dog who is there to remind us that if we are to practise the Christian virtues of charity and humility, we must extend our sympathy to all natural functions, even those which disgust us.[10]

This is early Rembrandt, but it is on the way to the reconciliation of those last self-portraits in which the decay of the flesh has been faced, noted and forgiven, and beauty returned.

> Art, driven out by the fork of philosophical seriousness, returns on a plane even higher than philosophy as the sacred art of right living in which the holiness of the divine order finds embodiment.[11]

A life shows us beauty along with ethics.

Dietrich Bonhoeffer's was one in which the Puritan virtues of obedience and renunciation played a determinative role. There was the leaving of respectable and promising careers; first, as an academic theologian, then, by allegiance to the unofficial Confessing Church, as a pastor with a stable field of work. Finally there was the renunciation of the claim to be thought of as a respectable Lutheran Christian by his implication in the attempt to assassinate Hitler – which entailed a further renunciation because it meant joining the *Abwehr* and so appearing to sell out on all that he had proclaimed in the thirties. Through all this comes the extraordinary relaxation and broad humanity of the letters he wrote from his cell in Tegel. There the author of *The Cost of Discipleship*, that modern classic of Puritanism, talks of this and that, of music and leisure, the benefits of reading and foreign travel. He looks for a Christianity which will meet secular man in his confidence and happiness and not just in his weakness and distress. He celebrates 'a beauty which is neither classical nor demonic, but simply earthly, though it has its own proper place. For myself, I must say that it's the only kind of beauty that really appeals to me.'[12]

These stories leave behind them a form of beauty which has nothing to do with dilettantism. It has allowed, by renunciation of itself, for God and for ugliness, and so become a seal of the covenant between heaven and earth. It has not avoided the worst or the best.

Two months after the entry in his journal with which we began Kierkegaard made another on his very last page:

> What pleases God even more than the praises of the angels is a man, who in the last lap of his life, when God is transformed as though into sheer cruelty, and with the cruellest imaginable cruelty does everything to deprive him of all joy in life, a man who continues to believe that God is love and that it is from love that God does this. Such a man becomes an angel. And in heaven he can surely praise God. But the apprentice time, the school time, is also the strictest time. Like a man who thought of journeying through the whole world to hear a singer who has a perfect voice, so God sits in heaven and listens. And every time he hears praise from a man whom he brings to the uttermost point of disgust with life, God says to himself, This is the right note. He says, Here it is, as though he were making a discovery.[13]

Parturient montes, nascetur ridiculus mus. 'Mountains will be in labour, the birth will be a laughable little mouse.'[14] At the end of all our toil the joke is happily on us. A world of common things is restored to us, 'simply earthly', each in 'its proper place' and precisely itself: the 'right note', the friends and relations, the work and the leisure – and the wonder. *

6
How goes it?

❧

'Den seligen Göttern wie geht's?' 'How goes it with the glorious gods?' The question is asked by Loge in scene two of *Das Rheingold*, the first part of the mythological tetralogy which Richard Wagner devised in the third quarter of the nineteenth century: at the time when analysis was impinging publicly on the divine myth of Christianity. Loge is not himself a fully-fledged god and glad not to be. He is the analytical faculty, the only intellectual in the whole vast musical saga, who turns himself into the dissolving-cum-creative element of fire. At the end of *Das Rheingold* the gods enter the fortress of Valhalla. Previously living at large in the world, they now have a place of their own. But they have got it built by a mixture of chicanery and denial of love (in the first instance, of course, to other people: the giants who built it). This will prove fatal to them in the end. Wotan himself, the most high god, finds his exultation in Valhalla modified by remorse and foreboding. He has used the ring, which gives power at the cost of love, to attain his end – and it is still at large and up for bids in the world. Loge watches as they go in to the castle

> They are hastening on to their end,
> Though they think they are great in their grandeur.
> Ashamed I'd be
> To share in their dealings;
> I feel a temptation
> To turn and destroy them;
> Change to flickering fire,
> and burn those great ones

who thought I was tamed,
rather than blindly
sink with the blind,
although they're so gracious and god-like!
I think that might be best!
I must consider:
who knows what I'll do?[1]

'Who knows what I'll do?' Will the fire of independent intellect consume away the fabric of religion for all but Bonhoeffer's 'few intellectually dishonest people on whom we can descend as religious' and 'last survivors of the age of chivalry?' Wagner's answer is more complicated and creative than nervous ecclesiastical reactions, to say the least. To cut a very long story short, Loge followed his inclination and became fire. As such he surrounded, at Wotan's command, the sleeping body of Wotan's daughter Brünnhilde, who disobeyed her father's orders (but not his deeper will) by taking love's side against law. She would be woken only by one brave enough to go through the fire ('let the reader understand'). As fire, too, Loge assisted in the reforging of the sword 'necessity' with which Siegfried killed the dragon who guarded the ring which, in passing to Siegfried, got at last into the hands of someone who was not interested in it. As fire, finally, he reached Valhalla and its divine inhabitants. But then he was fire, at the service not of Wotan's exhausted power, but of Brünnhilde's forgiving and redeeming love. The *Ring* cycle turns on a transferring of initiative – from power, however benevolent, to love, however betrayed. Only so is the ring's curse undone. Along with this, the human characters in the drama take more of a determinative part from the subhuman and superhuman ones. Wotan himself had willed it so. Divinity's ultimate achievement is the burning immolation of self-giving love for the human.

That is how it goes with the glorious gods. And the critical Loge has played his part. At the very least, Wagner's drama is a stupendous footnote to the story of Christianity in the last hundred years, whether institutional or individual. In theology there has been a momentous turning from thinking of God as omnipotent in heaven (Valhalla) to thinking of him as love in action on earth. As power has lost credit and credibility because it limits and excludes, love has emerged as the saving possibility and the one thing needful because it liberates and includes. It alone promises deliverance from the curse of Wagner's ring: power got by renouncing love. Books have marked the way, with the sensitive sophistication of John Oman's critique of omnipotence in *Grace and Personality*[2] or the blunt plain-speaking of John Robinson's *Honest to God*.[3]

Lives have marked it too. Albert Schweitzer took the most vigorous and acute critical mind of his generation from work on the New Testament to work on diseased bodies in Central Africa; Dietrich Bonhoeffer, his naturally Olympian temperament into the eye of a political storm and meditation on the ordinary things of life; Dag Hammarskjöld, the mystical heart into international affairs. Such examples move us more than the most valiant attempts in systematic or institutional theology. Their affecting power is the more striking for carrying through in an age when critical knowledge, being greater in extent if not in depth than ever before, makes impossible the allegations of faultless heroism or sanctity made on behalf of yesterday's worthies. This absence of pedestals has the daunting beneficial effect of making clear that such people are not magic but just people – and so something of their sort is possible for, and required of, us. The last chapter tried to indicate a few common or garden areas where it is required and possible. It seems from them that individual experiment is at present far more likely to deliver the goods than grand corporate edifices. It is a matter of phases, of 'everything in its time and a time for everything', but then good timing is arguably life's basic art. Cathedrals stupefy their modern visitors into wistful admiration. 'They don't build like that any more,' they say. As a matter of fact they do, if not more superbly, but more for scientific experiment at Cape Canaveral than in religion, where it is the day of small things – and woe to him who despises it! A cathedral is, after all, the temporary solidifying of the experimental work of a host of individuals into a totality, and is not morally unambiguous in its exhibition of corporate power. The integration which it once achieved is now, as long ago in New Testament times, a task of individual discipleship. When cathedrals (metaphorical or actual) serve that, they have a future as well as a past.

The monolithic power of the great corporation, Kierkegaard's 'Christendom', belongs in the debit column of a rough and ready stock-taking of contemporary Christianity. It has been spent. If Kierkegaard has any good news for us it is that we should not mourn for long over its passing, though a proper respect for its unequalled achievements prevents us from dancing on its grave. Valhalla's day is done, and it is noticeable that the Vatican, one of its last surviving earthly manifestations, seems to serve the general public best as an incongruously grandiose backdrop for an engagingly natural human figure: John XXIII with his peasant warmth, John Paul I with his jokes. It is, again, the man whom we want to know about; not just out of peephole curiosity, but to discover what goodness is possible in a human being now that we are less awed by the historical fancy-dress of robes of office. The gigantic apparatus gives little such help. Nor will attempts to recreate its reassuring atmosphere on the small scale of the religious enclave get us very far unless that is open, in a way quite new to it, to the individual's search for a just critique of his failure and for a sense of his own value – any individual's, not just one who likes church. If such a group is really the body of Christ, then it has to be a body so interested in those outside it that it is ready to be handed over to them. For the heart of Christianity is in that perilous movement.

It is ritually rehearsed in the eucharist and presented in the myth of the descent of divine being, in Christ, to the lowest depths of the world to redeem and divinize the entirety of human nature and nature. *Tu ad liberandum suscepisti hominem.* 'Thou tookest upon thee, to deliver (him), man.' Now we who believe in it know that this sort of language is mythological. Can we go on believing in it? We have long known that there were myths, but always thought that they were other people's. Ours were facts.

We did not like to think of them as 'doctrines felt as facts' because that discovers a crack in the foundations of the fabric, separating two things where we supposed there was one. Then we are tempted to ignore the discovery, with a fear which can always be paraded as piety, or down tools and walk away in a disappointment which can always be mistaken for honesty. It would be better if we paused first and took stock of what we have lost and what still remains for us to get on with. It will involve an attempt to grapple with Bonhoeffer's question of who Christ is for us today.

In the yesterday of the church's institutional heyday he was the crown and keystone of that magnificent structure, the integrating apogee of its authority. For some of his more adventurous disciples he was something else: for St Francis and the Langland of Piers Plowman a poor man, for mystics like Julian of Norwich a secret love hidden in the heart of all things. But these were minority reports. In the corridors of power and the places where Christianity's big business got done he was supreme authority, and as such stood above mankind on a pedestal of myth and fact monolithically integrated. There was heaven and from there he ruled, delegating to the church's officials authority to keep order. And if, like their archetype, Dostoyevsky's Grand Inquisitor, they used it to commit atrocities, they also used it to stop worse befalling and there was much sense in heeding the advice to

> Always keep a hold of nurse
> For fear of finding something worse

– as Martin Luther discovered too late when his dismissal of the nurse resulted in civil rebellions and religious freak-outs. In Wagnerian terms, the church as Valhalla had the ring of world-dominion. It was as well that she had, in view of some of the other contenders for it, but the ineluctable power of its curse was worked out in some terrible denials of love.

For the church the ring was its all-but perfectly integrated dogma of Christ. Worked out of the raw materials of the

New Testament, it made him the divine regent over human affairs. By right of perfect divinity and perfect humanity, Jesus Christ was Lord of All. This, in some form, is still the heart of Christianity from which this book has drawn constantly or round which it has circled endlessly. But the phrase 'in some form' is all-important, because it seems very unlikely that we can nowadays believe it in quite the same form. When we say 'Jesus Christ is Lord of All' we are not, as the medieval popes did, running a parallel or rival candidate to the Emperor's world-dominion. We do not share the triumphant militancy of the crusaders or even the four-square Victorian missionaries who followed the flag of empire. Very likely we mean something much closer to the minority reports of those old days.

Our title to this rests not only in a swerve in the undertow of the religious heart's affections and imagination. It rests also on the work of critics who have discovered a flaw in the fashioning of the authoritative ring of christological dogma. Their work on the New Testament has taken us back to the rawer materials from which it was beaten. An increase in scientifically historical objectivity – not complete, but enough to give the distance for some sort of objective view – has enabled them to see these documents more in their own terms, less through the established lens of the creeds. They were not just raw materials. Each of them was a theology in itself to be understood on its own, and not later, terms: which do not make it redundant. Diversity of doctrine has been discovered under apparently well-founded monolithic uniformity. Stories of various kinds, realistic and abstract, legendary, mythological, historical and in mixtures of these, under the majestically static edifice: things that move under the apparently unmoved and immoveable. It is akin to the physicists' discovery of a whirling dance of atoms informing the apparent solid stability of matter. Having made this discovery about Christian origins we are free to prefer the diverse movement to the unified stability and we are free to ask how the one got changed into the other.

The answer seems to lie in a confusion of categories made by the post-New Testament theologians of the

church. We can see it, but they could not. It was slight
and utterly excusable, but a flaw all the same. As
Christianity became the unifying religion of the ancient
West, the pressure on it to unify itself was intense and
irresistible. Otherwise it could not perform its new,
honorific and very important ordering job. Under this
pressure stories which move and tease the spirit were
transformed into dogmas which hold and restrict it. Instead
of being seen on their own terms, they were hammered
into another. And the transformation was sincerely believed
to be perfectly legitimate. The stories were seen as entirely
factual, and as unified by being so, and so it was proper
to deduce doctrine from them. They had crossed a line
without knowing it. The gospel of John, in particular, was
high on the agenda of their discussion and they believed
it to be an exact record of what Jesus had said and done.
So in their high doctrines of Jesus they were doing no
more than explicating what he had done and what he had
said.[4] It was a mistake only in the retrospect which we
get from clearer distinction between myths and facts, any
kind of story and any kind of doctrinal theory – and so
a kind of mistake well known and readily forgiven in any
field of developing knowledge. Just as Newton could not
have done otherwise or better than he did with his theory
of gravity, and took it for a law for ever (but Einstein has
taught us better, with his aside, 'Newton, forgive me!'),
so they could not have done otherwise or better than they
did with their theory of Christ, and took it for a law for
ever. And it served the imperative need of the time for
the kind of solidly unified centre, the definite and capacious
pot, the ring which a religion needs to establish itself.

But now the need has changed. The church as institution
is not looked to for the establishment of world order as
it was by Constantine. It is, in any case, in no state to
answer the call if it came. It finds its vocation more
amongst those who get a rough deal from it: the prisoners
of conscience, the have-nots, the dissatisfied prosperous.
Christ is with Mother Teresa down among the lost people
rather than at the apex of an intellectual or political
pyramid. Perhaps he will emerge there later (eschatologi-

cally, say the theologians of hope), but now his business is elsewhere.

The need is for a story to live rather than a dogmatic structure to maintain, for some kind of a map to move by rather than for a palace which we would not or could not settle in. The stories prised away from under the structure of doctrine and separated, temporarily at least, from it, come into their own to answer the need. And not least myth, because it is a story of everyman and for everyman. It never happened historically exactly as it says; it is always happening, or could happen, something like it says. In other words, it is not so much to be revered in a single incarnate instance which is not ours, as to be done in many incarnate instances which are ours. Discipleship is its only form of maintenance. The last chapter was an attempt to explore some such instances. And this whole book has been about the Christian myth of divine descent into its opposite out of love, an attempt to find out what that would mean for us today.

The thrust of its meaning, its historical business, is to get us to love our neighbour in the light of a God who moves to love us both. The good news is both that this myth itself drives us into this kind of relativity, and that the recognition of the category of myth, which separates it a little from authoritative dogma, actually helps with this. Once, when we were adolescent perhaps, we thought that love meant subsuming and subjugating other people under our own imaginative story about ourselves and God. Now, having come slightly more of age, we listen and hear other people saying that they each have an imaginative story of their own to tell, that they will not consider themselves properly loved if it is not appreciatively heard. 'Love me love my myth. Sit light enough to your story to understand mine and I will return that basic compliment.' And if this plea is heard, the ultimate myth of Christ as the man, and the divinity, for others is on the verge of achieving another historical instance. For it continually hovers over the dark waters of history only to wait for an opportunity to dip into them and be baptized into new historical life. When Jesus dined with publicans and sinners

who were too disreputable, or intelligent, or dangerous to
be accommodated in the most majestically triumphant
sectional interest, when his body was handed over and
given away because that is what bodies are for and because
our individual bodies are all that we have to do it with,
when that ecclesiastical symbol becomes a historical deed
somewhere inside or outside church, then it has achieved
its purpose. And we are a little nearer to seeing that
everything that lives is holy.

Notes

Chapter 1

1. Dr Norman betrayed no knowledge of the historical dubiety of this gospel, nor indeed of the implications raised by the application to the New Testament of the sort of historical criticism he himself deployed elsewhere.
2. G. F. Woods, *A Defence of Theological Ethics*, Cambridge University Press 1966, p. 65.
3. Origen, *Contra Celsum* 7.9.
4. An outstandingly ludicrous and horrible example was reported in *The Observer* on 21 January 1979: President Macias Nguema of Equatorial Guinea, whose terrorism vies with Idi Amin's and who calls himself *el unico miraglo*, the unique miracle.
5. Dietrich Bonhoeffer, *Letters and Papers from Prison. The Enlarged Edition*, edited by Eberhard Bethge, SCM Press 1971, pp. 278–82.
6. Hilaire Belloc, 'The Example', *Cautionary Tales for Children*, Duckworth 1974.
7. In *Phoenix*, Heinemann 1936, pp. 724–30. The whole short essay should be read because it is as important as Bonhoeffer's letter of 30 April 1944, and more vividly entertaining to the same end.

Chapter 2

1. C. G. Jung, *Answer to Job*, Hodder and Stoughton 1965, p. 159.
2. C. G. Jung, *Memories, Dreams and Reflections*, Fount Books 1967, pp. 363f.
3. See M. F. Wiles, 'Myth in Theology', in *The Myth of God Incarnate*, edited by John Hick, SCM Press 1977, 148–66, and C. Hartlich and W. Sachs, *Die Ursprung des Mythosbegriffes*, J. C. B. Mohr, Tübingen 1952.
4. See E.Shaffer, *Kubla Khan and the Fall of Jerusalem. The Mythological School in Biblical Criticism and Secular Literature*

1770–1880, Cambridge 1975, for a full and lively treatment.

5. C. G. Jung, *Memories, Dreams and Reflections*, p. 163.

6. Edmund Leach, *Lévi-Strauss*, Fontana Books 1974, p. 54, quoting Schniewind in *Kerygma and Myth*, ed. H. W. Bartsch, SPCK 1953.

7. Shakespeare, *A Midsummer Night's Dream*, V, 1.

8. In *The Myth of God Incarnate*, SCM Press 1977, and *Jesus and the Gospel of God*, Lutterworth 1978.

9. See H. W. Bartsch, 'The Present State of the Debate', in *Kerygma and Myth* II, SPCK 1962, pp. 1–47.

10. See James Barr, *Fundamentalism*, SCM Press 1977, *passim*.

11. *Speculations*, ed. H. Read, Routledge and Kegan Paul 1954, p. 51.

12. See Keith Thomas, *Religion and the Decline of Magic*, Penguin Books 1978, p. 123.

13. See J. D. G. Dunn, *Unity and Diversity in the New Testament*, SCM Press 1977.

14. Stephen Sykes, *The Integrity of Anglicanism*, Mowbrays 1978.

15. Stevie Smith, 'How Do You See?', *Collected Poems*, Allen Lane: The Penguin Press 1975.

16. Pierre Teilhard de Chardin, *Le Milieu Divin*, Fount Books 1964, pp. 95f.

Chapter 3

1. T. S. Eliot, 'Little Gidding', *Four Quartets*, Faber 1943, pp. 50f.

2. W. B. Yeats, 'He Wishes for the Cloths of Heaven', *Collected Poems*, Macmillan 1950.

3. I Kings 22. 34–37.

4. 'Of Ceremonies, Why Some be Abolished and Some Retained', *The Book of Common Prayer*.

5. Keith Thomas, *Religion and the Decline of Magic*, Penguin Books 1978, p. 192.

6. David Martin, 'Profane Habit and Sacred Usage', *Theology* 82, March 1979, pp. 83–95.

7. In Schoenberg's opera *Moses and Aaron*.

8. D. H. Lawrence, 'Pax' (a liturgical title!), in *Complete Poems*, Heinemann 1974.

9. It is a weakness of Karl Rahner's splendid *Theological Investigations*, Darton, Longman and Todd (16 volumes so far), that in them he calls the church the arch-symbol or arch-sacrament.

10. But not in Luke, who saves this for the Acts of the Apostles.

11. Wilfred Owen, *Collected Poems*, edited by Edmund Blunden, Chatto and Windus 1963, pp. 35, 82. For his Christianity see

Jon Stallworthy, *Wilfred Owen: A Biography*, Oxford University Press 1975.
  12. Christopher Hill, *Economic Problems of the Church*, Oxford University Press 1956; id., *The World Turned Upside Down*, Penguin Books 1976; id., *Milton*, Faber 1978, etc.; Keith Thomas, *Religion and the Decline of Magic*, Penguin Books 1978.
  13. Henry Reed, 'Naming of Parts', in *A Map of Verona*, Cape 1970.
  14. The General Thanksgiving in *The Book of Common Prayer* and the final chorus in T. S. Eliot, *Murder in the Cathedral*, Faber 1935, pp. 85–8.
  15. Geoffrey Lampe, *God as Spirit*, Oxford University Press 1977, p. 23.
  16. See W. H. Vanstone, *Love's Endeavour, Love's Expense*, Darton, Longman and Todd 1977, for an essay in pantheism steeped in divine human suffering.

Chapter 4

  1. The conviction informs C. F. D. Moule's essay 'The Christ of Experience and the Christ of History', *Theology* 81, May 1978, pp. 164–72; the question was aired in a letter from Alan Bill, *Theology* 80, May 1977, pp. 206f.
  2. Hans Conzelmann, *The Theology of St Luke*, Faber 1960 (the title of the German original was *The Middle of Time*).
  3. John Milton, 'On Time'.
  4. C. F. D. Moule, 'Through Jesus Christ our Lord: Reflections on the Use of Scripture', *Theology* 80, January 1977, pp. 30–6.
  5. Louis MacNeice, 'Autumn Journal IX', *Collected Poems*, Faber 1966, pp. 118ff.
  6. D. E. Nineham, *The Use and Abuse of the Bible*, Macmillan 1976, reissued SPCK 1978.
  7. T. S. Eliot, 'Little Gidding', *Four Quartets*, Faber 1943, p. 51.
  8. E. Busch, *Karl Barth – His Life from Letters and Autobiographical Texts*, SCM Press 1976, p. 409.
  9. T. S. Eliot, 'Ash Wednesday', II.1.
  10. John 19.22.
  11. John Higgins, *The Making of an Opera*, Secker and Warburg 1978.
  12. T. S. Eliot, *Murder in the Cathedral*, Faber 1935, p. 86.

Chapter 5

  1. S. Kierkegaard, *The Last Years. Journals 1853–1855*, edited and translated by R. Gregor Smith, XI[1] A248, pp. 101f. The nexus of thought and events in Kierkegaard's last years is narrated in Josiah Thompson, *Kierkegaard*, Gollancz 1974.
  2. At least, Kierkegaard thought it necessary. As he was

dying, his friend Boesen invited him to moulfy the harshness of
his attack on the church, but he refused: 'otherwise it doesn't
do any good. It has to burst like a bombshell. Do you think I
ought to tone it all down, first of all wake people up and then
calm them down? How can you want to confuse me like that? . . .
You must not forget that I have seen everything from the
inmost centre of Christianity; it's all very poor and clumsy. . .
It pleases me so much that you've come here. Thank you, thank
you' (Thompson, *Kierkegaard*, p. 233).

3. Graham Greene, a letter published in the *New York Times*
Sunday Magazine in Spring 1978. I do not have a more exact
reference.

4. Karl Rahner, *Theological Investigations* 14, Darton, Longman
and Todd 1975, p. 110 and *passim*.

5. W. H. Auden, 'Friday's Child: in memory of Dietrich
Bonhoeffer', in *Homage to Clio*, Faber 1960, p. 77.

6. This view is not popular among scholars nowadays, who
can appeal to A. D. Nock's essay in *Essays on the Trinity and the
Incarnation*, edited by A. E. J. Rawlinson, Longmans 1928, with
its relentless tendency to play down the connection, supported
by vast learning. But if the reader separates the learning from
the tendency he is left with a strong sense of Paul and the
mystery religions sharing the same world – and of Nock's
struggle to minimize it.

7. An opera with words by Hugo von Hofmannstal and music
by Richard Strauss.

8. W. H. Auden, 'Poems 1936–1939, XVII', in *The English
Auden*, ed. Edward Mendelsohn, Faber 1977, p. 228.

9. S. Kierkegaard, *Journals 1853–55*, ed. R. Gregor Smith,
Collins 1965, p. 350.

10. Kenneth Clark, *Rembrandt and the Italian Renaissance*, John
Murray 1966, p. 12.

11. Hans Urs von Balthasar, *Word and Revelation*, Herder 1964,
p. 129.

12. Dietrich Bonhoeffer, *Letters and Papers from Prison*, SCM
Press 1971, p. 239.

13. Kierkegaard, *Journals 1853–55*, pp. 368f.

14. Horace, *Ars Poetica* 139.

Chapter 6

1. Richard Wagner, *The Ring of the Nibelung*, translated by
Andrew Porter, Faber 1977, pp. 70f.

2. John Oman, *Grace and Personality* (1917), Fount Books 1960.

3. John A. T. Robinson, *Honest to God*, SCM Press 1963.

4. It is noticeable nowadays how any hint that the gospel of
John is historically veracious is swooped upon eagerly by
conservative theologians who are anxious to preserve Christendom's ancient monolithic authority.

Index